Stepping Out of It & Getting On with It

Stepping Out of It & Getting On with It

Pamela Bone

Deborah

God Bless You

Pamela Bone

iUniverse, Inc.
New York Lincoln Shanghai

Stepping Out of It & Getting On with It

Copyright © 2008 by Pamela R. Bone

All rights reserved. No part of this book may be used or reproduced by any means, graphic, electronic, or mechanical, including photocopying, recording, taping or by any information storage retrieval system without the written permission of the publisher except in the case of brief quotations embodied in critical articles and reviews.

iUniverse books may be ordered through booksellers or by contacting:

iUniverse
2021 Pine Lake Road, Suite 100
Lincoln, NE 68512
www.iuniverse.com
1-800-Authors (1-800-288-4677)

Because of the dynamic nature of the Internet, any Web addresses or links contained in this book may have changed since publication and may no longer be valid.

The views expressed in this work are solely those of the author and do not necessarily reflect the views of the publisher, and the publisher hereby disclaims any responsibility for them.

ISBN: 978-0-595-47186-7 (pbk)
ISBN: 978-0-595-91465-4 (ebk)

Printed in the United States of America

In memory of my Father, Joe Louis Robinson, Sr., (1939–2006). May your legacy of giving to others and service to all continue to live on through your family.

You are my hero!

Contents

Introduction ix
Chapter 1	The Beginning of a Season 1
Chapter 2	Moving to the Northwest 9
Chapter 3	Back to the ranks of the Employed 14
Chapter 4	Girlfriends 18
Chapter 5	Struggling to stay afloat 22
Chapter 6	The First Revelations 29
Chapter 7	My Open Heart to Surgery 35
Chapter 8	Southward Bound 42
Chapter 9	Déjà Vu: Here we go again 46
Chapter 10	Masquerade 51
Chapter 11	Awakenings 57
Chapter 12	A Leap of Faith 61
Chapter 13	Dad's Home Going 66
Chapter 14	God's Divine Mercy 71
Chapter 15	The Consumption of Grief 77
Chapter 16	Rebirth: The Road to a new Beginning 81

Introduction

I'm Pamela Robinson Bone. My family and friends simply call me "Pam." I am a 44 year old mother of two girls, and a special education paraprofessional at Kincaid Elementary School in Marietta, Georgia. Although my post-secondary education and formal training is not in the field of Special Education, it is near and dear to my heart. Working with children who have special needs, and raising a daughter with cerebral palsy has become my passion. I sincerely believe that every child is unique in his or her own way, no matter their ability or disability.

I began to write my story over two years ago while going through a marital separation and dealing with the sudden illness of my father. Writing was comforting and provided me with peace in the middle of all the turmoil. It is an experience in self-examination for who I am, what I am, and my evolution into what I have become. It is also an expression of my deepest thoughts and fundamental beliefs. A testimony, if you will, of Gods love and a doctrine to guide and assist others crying out for help.

The road has been long and the journey tough, but I continue to travel and take it day by day. Come along with me as I share the story of my life, and I trust that you will gain sustenance from the words on these pages.

1

The Beginning of a Season

On January 5, 1997, Lauren Nichole Bone was born into this world. Lauren weighed two pounds and eleven ounces, and was three months premature. The Lord had blessed me with my second bundle of joy. My life, my world, everything changed that Sunday evening, and nothing would ever be the same.

I woke up Sunday morning not as I usually had with my baby, whom I would later name Lauren, kicking inside of me, but instead feeling solemn. I thought that I was just having mood swings which are normal during pregnancy, but by early afternoon I noticed that Lauren had not been moving much at all. I had a doctor's appointment the next day, my seventh month check up, so I was not too alarmed. Mareva, my daughter who was four at the time, and I went to visit my grandparents and parents that afternoon. Mareva is named after her great-aunt on her dad's side of the family. I don't know the meaning of her name just that it is of Cherokee origin. I fell in love with the name immediately upon hearing it, and knew that this would be the name of my first born child, a special name for an extra special person. Our visit to my grandparents' home was uneventful, and I felt fine as we played kick ball in my parent's back yard.

Later that evening after arriving home I remember watching television and having a familiar sensation come over me. I was having contractions. One came and went, then another, and by the third I said, "No, this is not happening." The pains were familiar since I had gone through this once before. The contractions were about five minutes apart so I knew that I needed to take action. I immediately called my doctor's office but since it was after hours and the weekend; I spoke to the nurse on-call. She told me to get to the hospital as soon as possible. My husband, Marcus, was working out of state at the time and had just left about a week earlier, so he was not available. I called my mom, who was not home at the time, so I called my sister but she wasn't home either. Since I felt well enough to drive myself to the hospital, I decided to do that instead of waiting for paramedics to arrive. I dressed Mareva, grabbed her some snacks, and got in my car headed to Huntsville Hospital in Huntsville, Alabama, the same place I was born decades ago.

Since it was Sunday evening there was not a lot of traffic on the road, so I got there in record time. I pulled up to the emergency entrance and got out of the car when suddenly a security guard appeared. He told me that I could not park my car at the entrance, so I said "Look, I am in labor," I handed him the keys, and told him to do whatever he wanted with my car. At that point the contractions were closer and closer together, I knew that something had to be done quickly; it was way too early for me to be having this baby.

I was rushed to Labor and Delivery and it seemed to take an eternity to get there. I managed to undress and make some needed phone calls before things got really hectic. I finally got in touch with my mom and my sister. They both rushed to the hospital to take care of Mareva and help me with the birth of my child. I was scared, but I did not want to alarm Mareva; it was just too soon for this birth to take place. In the back of my mind, I remembered reading passages in books about premature births, and the difficulties which ensue. The nurses were working hard by injecting me with a drug in hopes of stopping, or at least slowing down labor, but to no avail. The baby was coming. Again, I thought it was too soon, would the baby even be alive? I was only 28 weeks pregnant.

I was in so much pain as there was no time for anesthesia, specifically an epidural the name that all women yell for when in labor. I had a nurse on one side of me, and on the other side there was Mareva trying to hide the fear that she must have been feeling. I was squeezing their hands fiercely, like there was no tomorrow. Finally, my mom and sister arrived. Mareva left the room with my sister, Beverly, and my mom took Mareva's place beside me. The doctor on-call arrived in my room, talked to a nurse, looked at my chart then made his way over to give me the news. There was no way that they could stop the labor. My baby would be born soon and there was no certainty of what would happen after the baby's arrival. He did not want to sugar coat it because he wanted me to be prepared. After approximately two hours this tiny, tiny little person arrived. I only got to see a glimpse of her before the team of nurses and doctors whisked her away. I did not hear her cry which mortified me, I could no longer feel my pain at that time, but I could certainly feel the pain of my little girl.

My mom tried to comfort me as the nurse's continued to perform post labor duties. All I wanted to do was see my baby and know that she would be alright. I was finally placed in a wheelchair and told that it was time for me to see her. Mom was by my side and a nurse on the other side. As we made our way down this very long corridor, the nurse tried to prepare me, but prepare me for what? She kept telling me that it was going to be okay, but I had no idea what she was talking about. I assumed that my baby was simply in an incubator being closely monitored. As the nurse pushed open double doors into the Neonatal Intensive Care Unit or NICU, my heart raced and my eyes welled with tears, for I had never experienced anything like that before. All I could see was this tiny, seemingly lifeless body hooked up to what appeared to be a vast amount of wires and monitors. Nothing could hold back the tears, for the pain that I felt at that moment was unlike any that I had ever felt in my life.

I kept asking myself what happened to my child, but I simply could not come up with any answers. Mother tried to comfort me, but there was nothing that anyone could say or do to make me feel better about this situation. Was it something that I either did or didn't do? What has just happened? What was going on? You can just imagine the thoughts that went through my mind. As I write down these words now, tears are welling up in my eyes as the memory of this night is both joyful and haunting.

After viewing my tiny infant, I was taken to my room where all I could do is wait for the doctor to update me as to my daughter's condition. Several nurses came in and out of the room to check my vital signs, etc—I even had someone contact me about naming my child. At that moment I really didn't care about my health, what her name would be or any thing else. Soon thereafter, the doctor on call came and paid me a visit. His face was subdued, so I knew it was not good news. The words that he uttered were "Your baby girl has about a 50% chance of survival." What did he mean "survival?" Was he crazy or worse yet, was he speaking of the same child, my child? I felt heaviness in my chest as though a ton of bricks were lying on my heart. I was in shock and wanted out of this nightmare. The doctor went on talking, and all I could do was see his lips move. I could not hear a thing, I simply wanted to trade places with this tiny being.

I immediately began praying, and I remember asking God to save my baby's life. I also made a promise or pact, if you will, asking him to save her life and in return I would devote my life to her and her well being. I recall saying that I would be by her side for an eternity or as long as she, or I was here on this earth. I recited this promise over and over again until I knew that the good Lord above heard, and would answer my prayer.

Several days went by and I finally received word that the worst was over and that she was out of immediate danger. I was advised that every day would be tough, and that she would remain in the hospital for months, or until the time of her original due date which was March 30th, approximately three months away. A nurse filled me in on what to expect, the daily practices and procedures in the NICU, a place that I would call home for the next few months.

By this time, Marcus finally arrived from his out of state work assignment and we named our daughter since she was finally out of the woods. My husband was only able to stay for a few days. Thus, the long haul began. I was left alone to deal. I became good friends with Lauren's primary nurse, Ada, who would later be a Godsend to me and my family. I made the daily trips to the NICU to sit with Lauren, talk to her, and try to bond as a mother and newborn are expected to do. Some days were good and some were bad. It's as if you took one step forward only to take two steps back. There were so many complications from her premature birth that it was frustrating to believe that you were on the road to recovery when bam, you were right back where you started.

Lauren developed a brain bleed, or ruptured blood vessel in her brain that caused very serious problems. A neurosurgeon was called upon to care for her, and to "tap" or extract the blood from her brain. The process of extracting the blood from her head went on for days, and I knew that something more had to be done. It was soon decided that Lauren would need a device called a shunt surgically placed in her head. This procedure would call for placing the device inside her brain to drain fluid out of her head, into her body, and out again.

I could not fathom the thought of this being done to my child. I knew that something had to be done, but not this, she had already been through so much pain and agony. I immediately called the pastor of my church, and asked him to visit with Lauren and me in the hospital. He came calling the next day, and I vividly remember him placing his hand on her tiny little head. He asked me to put my hand on his, and I complied. The nurses surrounding us ceased what they were doing, and my Pastor and I bowed our heads as he began to pray.

His prayer was not that Lauren be healed from this present crisis, but that the Lord's will be done. He asked that God touch this tiny being, to give her strength, to walk and stand beside her and most importantly to hold her during this critical time in her life. He also prayed that I would find comfort in his word and that I would learn and continue to walk by faith. His prayer was very inspirational as he is a true man of God.

I came and went that day knowing that the next would be a very difficult one. I remember talking to my mom that evening and expressing concern over what the procedure and outcome would bring. She simply told me, as she often did, "Have faith in God that his will be done." She would always tell me to have faith, that God does not make mistakes. Later in my life I would come to realize these words and find comfort in them as well.

I went about my duties for the evening; putting Mareva to bed, ironing, etc—As I prepared to get ready for bed, I prayed all of my cares and concerns to our heavenly father, and Lauren was at the top of the list. I stayed on my knees that evening and prayed all night long. I eventually came to terms with what would happen the following morning.

The day broke so I went on, business as usual. I prepared breakfast, and dressed Mareva and myself. We headed out the door to my parents' house since mom was to look after Mareva for the day. Upon entering the front door all I could hear was my mom calling my name, "Pam, Pam, come here." I sensed a nervousness or urgency about her voice, so I was leery to go upstairs to find out what she wanted. As soon as I entered her room she blurted out, "You need to call the hospital, now!" I looked at her with bewilderment; I asked her who had phoned and at what time. She then replied that a nurse in the NICU had called about 20 minutes earlier, and that it was imperative that they get in touch with me as soon as possible.

There was really no time to ask any further questions, so I picked up the phone and dialed the number. The hospital switch board operator answered, and I promptly asked for the NICU. I was put on hold for a few seconds; however, it seemed like an eternity. I did not recognize the voice of the young lady who answered, so I simply identified myself and stated the purpose of my call. She asked me to hold for a moment while she retrieved someone who could assist me. Finally a familiar voice rang out in my ear; it was Lauren's nurse, Ada.

She had become a very important person in my life in that she had provided me with comfort and hope. She would always greet me with the most welcoming and engaging smile, all the while being stern and diligent as a mother would be in dealing with her child. Ada had been a nurse in the NICU for decades, so her experience in dealing with frightened and anxious parents such as me had become invaluable to Huntsville Hospital. Ms. Ada, as I often referred to her, was a soft spoken woman with a quiet demeanor. She knew what to say and how to say it; she had simply become my rock, and truly a blessing. I trusted her with my child's life, and I paid close attention to all she had to say.

We exchanged pleasantries, and then she continued on to say that the surgery had been "cancelled." I asked her to repeat herself because I knew she didn't say what I had prayed, wished and hoped for. Yet, again she said that the surgery had been cancelled. I remember asking her, "Are you sure it has been cancelled and not postponed?" Her reply was an emphatic, "Yes, the surgery has been cancelled and is no longer needed." She then went on to explain that Lauren had been taken earlier that morning for a CT scan, an x-ray that was needed in preparation for the surgery. Upon viewing the CT scan it was discovered that Lauren no longer had a problem, the bleeding had ceased and there was no further evidence of any other problems with her head. I was totally amazed, and I immediately started saying "Thank you Lord, Thank you Lord." This was truly a miracle and a blessing from God. How could I not praise his name for he had delivered my baby from yet another ordeal? He had healed her tiny little head.

Mother was looking at me with much anticipation and excitement. She was literally bursting at the seams to find out what was going on. I thanked Ada for the wonderful news, and told her that I would be there in an hour to visit with Lauren and hung up the phone. Mother kept asking me what was happening, so I told her to sit down for the news. She was very anxious for me to begin speaking, so I jumped right in and told her that the surgery had been called off. She was stunned, and a look of relief shined in her eyes. I continued to fill her in on all of the details while tears streamed from her face. We embraced and said a prayer.

From that day on it appeared that Lauren was finally on the road to recovery. There were days in which she required blood transfusions since she was so tiny and anemic. One day in particular, Ada was waiting for me at the door before one of my morning visits. She told me that she had to tell me something very important. She went on to say that she had to shave off a section of Lauren's hair from her head. Before I could utter a word she continued on to say that Lauren needed yet another transfusion, and that they had run out of injection sites to use since she had needed so many. I understood why this had to be done. I just felt for my baby, and all that she had endured in her brief time on this earth.

Finally, there were no more major hurdles to cross. Things seemed to turn around for the better. Lauren began to thrive as she gained the necessary weight to be released from the hospital. Two and a half months had elapsed from the day of her birth, and I was finally able to take my baby home with me. I would be able to care for my own child, feed her, bathe her, hold her, all of the experiences that a new born and mother share.

The doctors, as well as Ada, tried to prepare me for the long road that Lauren and I would soon embark upon. Since Lauren was so premature, there would certainly be developmental delays, or some type of disability. They went on to explain that she would be slow in reaching certain milestones that is expected of a child, such as rolling, sitting, grasping at objects and even walking. One doctor went even further to say that she may never reach any of these milestones at all. There would be countless visits to doctor's offices, hospitals, even the possibility of surgery loomed over the horizon. They all wanted me to be prepared for the journey, and they gave it to me straight.

    Ada pulled me to the side and told me to listen very carefully to what she was about to say. She told me that Lauren was God's "very" special child, and that he had chosen me for her care and well being. She continued to say that God "favors" me in that he has given me this charge in life, and not to take it lightly. She also added that everything and everyone has a purpose in life, and that nothing happens by chance. Everything in life has already been ordained and ordered by God. She told me to never, ever ask the question, "why me?" and to never feel sorry for myself, for this charge that I have been given will often be difficult, but that God will always be by my side. I had never realized the blessing that had been given to me until now, and I thanked Ada for all that she had done for us. I did not say good-bye to her, but so long since I knew in my heart that I would be seeing her once more.

2

Moving to the Northwest

It was a rainy, cold, damp and dreary day as we arrived in Seattle, Washington. I could not believe that it was the end of June, summer time, or so I thought. I would soon find out that weather in this region is not typical at all; it's either raining or cloudy, well most of the time.

Marcus had begun work for The Boeing Company one month earlier, so he was somewhat familiar with the area; however this was my first trip to the "Great Northwest." It was beautiful: snow capped mountains, lush green trees, crystal clear lakes, and the city skyline was breath-taking. To see Mount Rainier and the Space Needle was monumental and breathing the fresh air was something to remember.

We settled in a city by the name of Mukilteo which is located approximately 25 miles north of Seattle. This area is comprised of great schools, and it was only a ten minute drive from Boeing. Mukilteo is a small, quaint, and quiet town. There was much history there, and a portion of it boarded the Puget Sound, which is a major waterway in the region. We would often take the ferry on the Sound to get to the bordering town of Whidbey Island.

Life was good. Marcus had a job that he seemed to enjoy and the girls were adjusting nicely. Mareva would start kindergarten in the fall, and I was excited to find out about programs for Lauren. We lived in a nice apartment complex, and we began to make friends. We met one couple in particular: Mitchell and Patricia. They also had two girls, one of which was Mareva's age. They were new to the area as well, so we were all finding our way together. It was nice having friends to "kick it" with, or so I thought!

Anyway, Mareva began attending kindergarten at a private institution. She had always wanted to go to school even when she was two years old. I can remember numerous times in which we were on our way to daycare, and she would see kids walking to school with their back packs, and she would ask, "Where are they going?" I would reply, "To school" and she would say, "I want to go to school with them." She was always interested in learning, and was an avid reader, so she needed the challenge that a private school would afford her. She needed that challenge so that she could go beyond the borders, and work at her own pace. Mareva is a gifted young girl, and God had blessed her with remarkable abilities.

With Lauren needing so much attention I opted to stay home with her, at least for the first year of her life. We had so many doctors' appointments during that first year; it took me no time at all to learn my way around the city.

I didn't particularly care for Lauren's pediatrician since she told me at the onset that Lauren would never walk. She was very pessimistic, and not a person whom I believed walked with faith. I turned a deaf ear to what I perceived as her ignorance, and simply let her know that I would do whatever I could to help my child reach her fullest potential.

Her office referred us to a program that catered to developmentally disabled children ranging from birth to three years of age. It was a therapeutic program that consisted of physical, speech, and occupational therapy. Lynn was the name of our physical therapist, and she was wonderful. She turned me on to a ton of resources in and around the Seattle area. She worked hard with Lauren and through her efforts we came to the realization that Lauren would face some very difficult challenges.

She was not able to sit up, roll over, pick up toys, all of the milestones that babies are expected to accomplish. She also developed a seizure disorder that was labeled "Infantile spasms." These "spasms" caused her tiny body to convulse and twitch. We were referred to a neurologist who administered tests such as an MRI, CT scan, video monitoring; you name it and he did it! After a two-day hospital stay to monitor Lauren and tape these occurrences, we were sent home with vials of medicine and syringes.

I was given the task of administering a shot daily to Lauren in an effort to control and subsequently stop the spasms. I had never been squeamish or fainted at the sight of blood, but this was totally different. I had to stick a needle into Lauren's tiny little thighs everyday for approximately six weeks. It was agonizing at first because she cried, and looked at me as if to say, "Why are you hurting me?" I tried to explain the need for the injections, because I knew in my heart that they were necessary. We both got through this, and her spasms ceased after only three weeks. Her doctor was surprised at how quickly the spasms subsided, and we rejoiced in getting through yet another hurdle.

Shortly after what I now call "phases" of health concerns, Lauren's neurologist called us back into his office for a follow up appointment. He showed me the pictures of Lauren's MRI; of course, I had no clue of what I was viewing. He went on to explain that Lauren had scarring of the brain, or in layman's terms, "brain damage." With the advances of technology, he could actually determine the age of the scarring. Lauren's brain damage had occurred while she was still in the womb.

Looking back, I remembered mom had told me that the umbilical cord had been wrapped around Lauren's neck when she was born. This cut off circulation to her brain, causing scarring in several areas. I went back to the night prior to Lauren's birth, and I vividly remember her turning so fiercely that it almost brought me to my feet. It felt as if she were doing summersaults in my stomach. I wasn't alarmed because she was always very active, even in the early stages of my pregnancy. Is this what happened to my little one?

Two months prior to Lauren's first birthday, she was diagnosed with Cerebral Palsy. Cerebral Palsy is defined as impaired muscular power, and coordination due to brain damage at or prior to birth. So, what would this mean for her? Would she ever be able to walk, talk, play, or sing a song? Those are the questions that I played in my head over and over again. What exactly would be her fullest potential, and what would be her quality of life?

This was the age of technology, so I got on the computer and researched cerebral palsy. I also purchased books so that I was completely knowledgeable of what we were facing, and I became an expert on the terminology. The words spastic, quadriplegic, postural muscles and high and low tone would become a part of my everyday vocabulary. These, among countless other words, help to describe a condition that affects an overwhelming number of children each year. Some cases are mild in that only fine motor skills are affected, while other cases are more severe, affecting fine and gross motor skills.

Lauren's cerebral palsy from first glance appeared to be severe in that the scarring in her brain affected her ability to walk, talk or grasp objects. She was categorized as a quadriplegic since she was unable to use her upper or lower extremities. Cerebral Palsy is not a disease in that it progresses or worsens; it is simply a condition or state of being. There is no cure for cerebral palsy, but one does learn to live with and compensate for those areas of the body that are most affected.

Did these recent events really mean that much? Did it matter that we now had a diagnosis for Lauren's disability? It was nice to have a name for her condition, but it did not define who my child was as a person. Her body may have been frail, but her soul and spirit were whole.

The next few months brought about learning, exploring and adjusting. Lauren did not like wide open spaces; she would always want to be held and cuddled. In fact, she disliked riding in her car seat when she was an infant. I would take Mareva to school as well as pick her up, and Lauren would cry the entire time, round trip. At first I thought that she would get accustomed to the rides, but she didn't and her screaming and crying became increasingly intense. I had come to the point where I dreaded these daily trips, and Lauren and I both would sob together in unison. I did not know what to do for her. Would everything in our lives be such a challenge? Would she eventually grow out of this, or would things become more difficult? All that I could do was live one day at a time, and try to make the best of our situation in spite of the day-to-day difficulties. So, I suffered in silence, something I became quite accustomed to doing. I had never in my life felt so much anguish and despair. I always felt on edge, and had a difficult time in coping with life as a whole.

I also felt so alone: as if God had punished me by giving me this gigantic burden. I was only thirty-four years old, and so very far away from my friends and family. I never thought of myself as being a strong and willful individual, so what was I going to do?

It took a lot of soul searching and tears for me to come to terms with what was now my life. I had to always plan for simple things, such as going to the grocery store, shopping trips, running to the dry cleaners and other such outings. Since Lauren could not walk, her mode of transportation was a wheelchair. The chair had to be disassembled or broken down to fit into the trunk of the car. Can you imagine having to lift it out of the trunk, and assembling it at every stop? Not to mention lifting and transferring Lauren all day, each and every day. This would most certainly be cumbersome for a man, but just think … I am a small-framed woman of modest height and weight. Lifting that chair several times a day was difficult and back breaking work, but I did whatever I had to do, whenever I had to do it.

All of this was new to me. I had never known of anyone with a disability much less taken care of someone with this condition. I did not know what to do or what to expect. I had to learn how to take care of this child who would be totally dependent upon me for every aspect of her life. I had no time to be selfish, no time for pity or self doubt. Was God preparing me for a higher calling? Was he testing my faith, my love for him, and the love for me and my child?

Was I mature enough emotionally to take care of Lauren? I had to be a grown up in every aspect of the word. My time belonged to her and Mareva, and selfishness was something that I had to surrender. I had to be responsible and diligent; in other words, I had to take care of business. I soon learned that I possessed virtues that I never knew existed. God was shaping me, molding me, and building my character. Of course, at the time I hadn't come to realize these truths, therefore, I did not welcome him and praise his name as I should.

God works with us through many ways, things and people. We simply have to be open to receive his goodness and mercy. I just needed to be still and listen to receive my blessings.

3

Back to the ranks of the Employed

Things were finally stable with Lauren as far as her health was concerned, so I pondered the idea of returning to work, something that I had done since I was a young girl of 14 years of age. I had a decision to make concerning when and where I would return to work. I received my Bachelors degree from Alabama A&M University in Huntsville, Alabama, and had been employed in the Mortgage Banking industry for over 15 years. I had aspirations of obtaining a Master's Degree in Business, and had previously taken a couple of courses on the graduate level. I had completed a Management Information Systems class just one month prior to Lauren's sudden arrival. Her birth and subsequent health problems had led me to postpone continuation of the program.

I had updated my resume' and searched the classified ads for a position as a loan processor, loan officer or underwriter. I had previously worked in all three positions and could perform each job well. After a couple of weeks I received a call from Full Spectrum Lending which is a division of Countrywide Home Loans. I had applied for a position as a Senior Loan Processor in the Bothell, Washington branch which was only about a half hour commute from home.

Full Spectrum is the sub-prime (B-D credit) division of Countrywide which caters to persons who have less than perfect or no credit at all. I loved these types of loans because they were not only a challenge, but our clients were so appreciative when their loans closed. I learned much about life while doing these types of loans. People would often lose their jobs, or have serious medical, or health issues which led to their inability to work and earn a living. It was not always those persons who simply did not pay their bills. These were people who got the news that they were terminally ill, or that they were being laid off of a job that they may have held for years. Most of the people that I encountered were decent, hard working folk.

I vividly recall one customer who lost her husband to a fatal illness. She had never worked, and had depended on her husband since he was the sole bread winner for the family. She was a mature lady, and they had been married for nearly half a century, so it was not easy for her to re-enter the work force. Her husband's death left her with little since he had a scant retirement account, and only enough life insurance to cover burial expenses. She was several months behind in her mortgage payments, and faced almost certain foreclosure if something was not done soon. This woman had no family to offer her assistance or to direct her next move, so it was incumbent upon me to do whatever I could to save her home. Luckily, this woman was blessed to have had enough equity in her home to pay off all of her debt, and still be able to afford her monthly mortgage payments.

I would encounter stories such as this on a daily basis, and often times I would go out of my way to offer a resolution. It was as if I felt their pain, and that I was going through their ordeal with them. How could you not feel their loss and despair? This was more that just a job for a lot of us working there. We would often put in extra long hours, meet or assist our clients at their closings, or offer a shoulder to lean on or an ear to simply listen.

My manager was a woman by the name of Noah, and she, like me, had been in the mortgage business for a number of years, and in several different states. She had also worked in several different capacities at numerous institutions, thus being very knowledgeable in the mortgage business. She was a nice person, but by the same token a no-nonsense person. Her purpose there was to make our branch number one in our region, and month after month she accomplished this goal.

All of my co-workers were cool, but there was one person in particular that I became very good friends with. Theresa was employed as a loan officer, and she was the first person that I met at Full Spectrum. She was very petite with dark flowing black hair. Theresa is of Vietnamese descent, and has a personality unlike any person that I have ever encountered. We quickly became friends and worked well together. Even though I was quite a few years older than she, we had a lot in common. Later on Theresa would become invaluable to me, and a great source of strength and support.

I quickly learned the ropes of the company and moved on to become a loan officer myself. I had never worked so hard or so long in my life. It was common to work on weekends, long nights during the week, and to take work home any given day of the week. I was learning a lot and on my way up in corporate America.

The company and its leadership changed over the next couple of years. There were periods of time when we flourished, and on the down side when we struggled to meet our monthly goals. Employees came and went, and there was constant change in the mortgage industry. It was a challenge to keep abreast of the various programs that were offered.

Theresa was promoted as our new branch manager, and her leadership skills were top notch. Our branch experienced success right off the bat, and we were always at the top of our region in purchase and refinance transactions month after month. Her work ethic was commendable and something to be respected. She led by example, and several of the employees mirrored the work that she tried so hard to implement. It was not always easy for her since she was very young. There were employees who did not like or respect the fact that they had to answer to someone who was ten to fifteen years their junior. This simply fueled her to work harder and harder, and I must say that she succeeded in every turn.

Our branch thrived initially, but we also experienced growing pains which was not uncommon. There are so many mortgage companies and lending institutions, that the turnover rate was significant with personnel moving from company to company. Our most productive time was when we worked together as a team, with employees who had been around one another for quite some time. The camaraderie was great, and we were successful in all of our endeavors.

I remained at this company and at this branch for a long period of time. I believed in what we were trying to accomplish for people. We provided a service, and knew that we were changing lives for the better. I appreciated all that I learned and experienced, but I knew that this was not what I wanted to do for the rest of my life. Even though I sometimes had to work long hours, I was comfortable there and I had settled into a pattern. My goal was still a Masters of Business degree, but I realized that this would be very difficult while working full-time with a family to boot.

What would be my calling in life? Would I soon find that something that I would enjoy doing? Would this something bring me great satisfaction and joy? Would it be my passion, and would it be significant to bring glory to God? The good Lord had placed me here for a reason, and as with all things nothing happens by chance. There is always a reason. I had learned much at Full Spectrum with the most important lesson being that of showing compassion to others. This job also provided lessons that I would carry with me throughout the rest of my life. I knew that I was good at dealing with people, and this experience was positive and irreplaceable. However, my destiny was still waiting for me out there in the world!

4

Girlfriends

There is a phrase in a song that states "Make new friends but keep the old, one is silver and the other's gold." Friendship and sisterhood go hand in hand, and when one finds a true friend that relationship should be nurtured and treasured. I was finally adapting to life in Seattle and making new friends. My friend Patricia cared for Lauren when I returned to work, so I would see her and catch up on things every day. She did not plan on working, so what a perfect scenario for her to keep my baby. She was a close friend, and I could depend on her to take good care of Lauren. Our families often got together for dinner; we celebrated our children's birthdays with one another as well as other special events in our lives. She and I would also have a "girl's night out" in which we dined, and frequented a movie theater. We became close, in that we confided our innermost thoughts with each other. I trusted her, and deeply believed in our friendship. She was my sister.

I soon met a remarkable woman by the name of Kim. She is a beautiful bi-racial woman, tall in stature with long and thick wavy hair. She and her family lived in our complex as well. Kim married a man of Chinese descent, and thus had four beautiful children, two girls and two boys. Her youngest boy and girl were a set of twins by the names of Quinn and Rebecca. Mareva and Rebecca were the same age, and therefore had a lot in common and became good friends. This friendship was one of the reasons Kim and I became so close. We were alike in many ways. She liked to keep a clean house, and she took care of her family really well.

Kim worked full-time at a banking institution, and her husband worked at Boeing. We would often see each other at the mailbox at which time we would engage in lengthy conversations. Like me, Kim had a strong sense of family, so it was refreshing to meet someone of the same caliber. It was also nice that she lived across the street from me, so if I ever needed anything she was just a stone's throw away. Her character was unyielding, and I knew I could count on her to do what she said she would do. Like the saying goes, "Her word was her bond and who she was."

Now, of course, there was dear Theresa from work. Theresa and I just gelled together like glue. It was almost as if we were cut from the same fabric. We both learned at an early age that you had to work hard to get what you wanted out of life, and we learned this lesson well. Theresa is a very intelligent young woman. She is also cunning and daring. She did not mind pushing the envelope when needed, and she was a perfectionist at every turn. Theresa is a survivor, and she always wants to win and to be on top. This work ethic would one day escalate her up the corporate ladder.

Theresa and I often shared our family histories with one another. Although we came from different cultures, our families instilled in us the same ethics when it came to work, family, and friends. It was ironic that Theresa and I began working at very early ages. Although we both grew up somewhat middle class, we still had to work for the things that we wanted; nothing was handed to us on a silver platter. We were both hard core in that we did whatever we had to do to strive, thrive, and survive. Theresa cared for her parents financially, and she was always generous with whatever she had. I don't know many young people in their twenties who would take on such a task. But she did it with pride and without seeking praise. What a strong sense of family! Theresa is a real gem.

What is in a name? Carmella is her name, what a beautiful and soft flowing name. I met Carmella at a cheerleading clinic that Mareva was attending along with her daughter Brianna. She had recently moved to the area from Portland and was working at an elementary school. Carmella is a petite, light skinned sista with a short cropped haircut. She would joke about going to the barber shop versus the beauty shop. Carmella often wore knee length black boots with high heels. This became her signature, and she would work it ever so gracefully. Carmella has a great sense of humor, and is very spiritual. Whenever we speak we never pass judgment on each other but instead offer good sound advice. Her friendship is easy and comforting. She has helped me with my girls, and is always willing to offer a helping hand. The one character trait that I adore in her is the fact that she is so eager and willing to help me with Lauren. It simply doesn't matter that she has to handle the wheel chair and other such cumbersome devices; she just wants to lend a hand.

I also have another wonderful woman in my life that I've known for years. She lived in the Los Angeles area, a place where I had lived in the late eighties. Although miles separated us physically, we were always in each others heart and minds. Lisa is more of a sister than a friend. We had known each other for over 15 years, and she had been through some heavy stuff in her life. These life experiences brought forth much wisdom to our relationship. The one thing that I remember about my girl Lisa is that she always had her hair laid, and the nails shaped and polished. Lisa is the mother of two, a girl and a boy. Her son was the youngest, and suffered from developmental disabilities of his own. This was one thing that we had in common, our children with special needs.

It was nice knowing someone whose journey was similar to my own. Lisa provided me with a wealth of information and resources. She also talked to me about having the strength to care for God's special children. She tried to prepare me for the future, and all of the obstacles that I would encounter. Her heart was big, and her compassion was huge. It did not matter that thousands of miles separated us; we would always pick-up where we left off. What a blessing she was to me and my life.

Of course, I have childhood friends whom I have known for what seems like all of my life. These are women with whom I had grown up with, attended the same schools, was on dance team with, and shared in the marvelous blessings of weddings as well as the births of our children. I have kept in touch as best I can with these women who mean so much to me, as they represent home base, stability and my beginning. Half of these sisters still reside in Huntsville, and while the other half is scattered over the country, we still get together when we visit home.

Some of these women are also my Sorors in that we belong to the same sorority, Alpha Kappa Alpha Sorority, Incorporated. My sorors are some of the finest women that God has fashioned. The sisterhood of this organization rivals any other out there, and I am proud and privileged to be a member of the ladies wearing the pink and green.

There is a saying that people come into our lives for a reason, a season or a lifetime, and that when you know which one it is, you will know what to do for that person. I wasn't quite sure who was a reason, a season or a lifetime, but one thing that I knew for sure is that at one point in time these women were all my friends, and my sisters in Christ.

5

Struggling to stay afloat

A most difficult time had arisen in the Bone household. My husband was laid off from his job at Boeing. He was a contractor, and not a direct employee therefore he was one of the first persons to lose their jobs. I was still working at Full Spectrum, so this meant that I had to step it up a bit since I was at this time the sole bread winner for my family. I often times worked 50–60 hours per week, all the while taking the kids to school, cooking, homework, getting the girls ready for bed, ironing for the next day, etc … My days began at 5a.m., and did not end until midnight or later. How could one person do so much? I really thought that my husband would help out more than he did, but it just did not happen. I think he was depressed over his job situation which manifested into his removal from our family, and its daily operations.

Every Friday night after putting the kids down for bed I would stay up to do the chores. Since I worked all week the laundry piled up, so I would have to stay up and wash about six loads of laundry. I had to clean, mop, vacuum, etc … the entire house. I did this work on Friday night, so that I would be free on Saturday to hang out with the girls, and this meant staying up until 3 or 4 a.m. Now, one would think that by having a husband temporarily out of work that some of this would be done by him, yeah right! My husband chose to go out with his friends on Friday nights. Our relationship deteriorated quite a bit during this time. I could not understand why he would leave, and always be gone. He was a husband and a dad, so why not be there with his family? Why not help me out, and work by my side?

Was he going through something other than the fact that he had been laid off? I was paying the bills and we always had food on the table, you

In spite of all the stress that I was going through at this time in my life, there was one incident that was a blessing. My friend Theresa knew what I was going through, how times were tough and finances lean. I spent so many hours with her at the office that she knew something was bothering me, so I confided in her. Right there on the spot she gave me a check in the amount of $1,000.00 dollars to use as I saw fit. It was not a loan, as she emphatically stated that it was a gift from a friend. I don't think that I had ever experienced such kindness from anyone outside of my family. I knew that she would be a lifelong friend.

While driving home one afternoon I remember having a near black out. This scared me so much that the next day I called my doctor and made an appointment. I was also experiencing chest palpitations while doing menial tasks such as running the vacuum cleaner. I would simply run out of air, start wheezing, and get really dizzy. My appointment day had arrived and my doctor asked me to describe a normal day. This is what I told him. I would wake up at 5 a.m. and get dressed, wake the girls, dress Lauren and make sure that Mareva was dressed. Then I would prepare breakfast and feed Lauren. After that I would drop Mareva off at school and Lauren at daycare. I would then arrive at work and stay until 6 p.m., after which I would go home and cook, feed Lauren, wash the dishes, assist Mareva with homework, and start running baths. I then would enjoy some down time with the girls before getting them off to bed. Once they were in bed, I would clean out book bags, iron clothes, and prepare the girls' lunches for the next day. Finally, I had some down time for my self which included a facial, brushing my teeth and rolling or wrapping my hair to prepare for bed. At last, I would be able to lay my head down on my pillow around 12 p.m. However, since Lauren was not able to turn her body or reposition herself other than her head, she would wake up during the night, and I would have to turn her over. I would be lucky if this happened only once each night, but sometimes it would be two or three times a night if she was having trouble sleeping.

I also went into detail about Lauren's disability, and pending surgery, my husband not working, and the long hours on the job. His reply was that I am stretched too thin, and stressed out to the max. He was simply know, things were being handled and taken care of. I tried to get him to talk to me, but he had never been very open with his feelings. He was the type of person to just sit back, and think that he could handle whatever came his way. He didn't need, or seek out advice from anyone. Not even me, his wife and partner.

We lost the closeness that we had once shared for one another. I was so busy trying to keep things working smoothly at home and taking care of the girls that I lost sight of taking care of "us." Caring for Lauren was a full-time job, it compared to caring for an infant in that I had to do everything for her, feeding, bathing, clothing her, positioning her, and playing with her. She was not able to do anything for herself, as she depended on others for everything. Parents look forward to the day when their children grow up, and get out on their own, but I will never experience such an occasion; Lauren will live with me for the rest of her life.

The fall of 2000 brought some disappointing news for Lauren, and our household as a whole. She was under the care of several specialists due to her cerebral palsy, one of which was an orthopedic surgeon. Lauren was diagnosed with having a dislocated left hip. She also needed to have soft tissue releases of the left hip, as well as the right. This meant major surgery to correct the problems with her hips. Since Lauren had limited movement, and mobility it was difficult to sense that she may have been in pain. I did not take this news very well. I was still in the mind frame of thinking, had I done things differently when I was pregnant, then maybe she would have been full term and free of any type of disability. Therefore, instead of coming to terms with her impending ordeal, and knowing that it was for the best, and that it would relieve any pain that she may be feeling. I opted to stress over the surgery, which lead to my own health declining.

I was under tremendous stress having to work overtime to pay the rent, bills, etc … since my husband was still out of work. I was also trying to be "Super Mom," by keeping the house spotless, cooking meals, laundering clothes, as well as taking the girls where they needed to go, such as doctor's appointments, therapy, etc … I asked my husband for help with Lauren but his reply was, "You are her mother and you should be able to take care of her." If that was not a big, fat red flag, then I don't know what was!

going to prescribe an anti-depressant drug for me, but thought that I should have a few minor tests performed before doing so. Since I was having chest palpitations, these tests were precautionary measures. He sent me to the hospital that afternoon with an order to have heart and lung function tests.

I arrived at the hospital and waited until they called my name. The technician asked me a few questions, then briefly described the procedure he was about to perform. The only thing I remember about that entire incident is lying there on a hard cold table, being injected with some type of solution, and looking at a monitor. He must have repeated this a few times before he told me to go and sit in the waiting area. I sat there for over an hour not knowing what was going on, or better still why I had to wait for what was described as a simple test.

A doctor emerged from the corridor and escorted me to her office. She asked me to sit down, and she told me that the test was abnormal. Before she could explain I blurted out "What do you mean abnormal?" She then proceeded to explain that the technician repeated the test to make sure he was not in error, since his findings were inconclusive. She continued to tell me that I "most likely" had some type of heart abnormality that would require further testing, as well as follow-up with a cardiologist. I simply could not believe what I was hearing; there is no way that anything could possibly be wrong with my heart. I knew that I had a touch of asthma which sometimes affected my breathing, but certainly nothing of this nature or magnitude.

How could this be happening to me? At this time I was only 38 years old, I never smoked, never drank. I was not overweight and I was in good physical shape. There was so much going on in my mind that I honestly do not remember how I got back to my car that evening. I was in a state of shock and I sat there in my car dazed by the news that was given to me. After sitting there in that dimly lit parking lot, I grabbed my cell phone and called my mom. I explained to her what had been going on with me, and that I was sent to the hospital for testing. I proceeded to tell her about the results and initial prognosis. She was absolutely speechless, since I had never had any serious health problems, other than a bout of pneumonia when I was twenty years old.

I began sobbing because I knew that this was serious. I just had a gut feeling. Of course, my mom being the caring, and nurturing person that she is, tried her best to comfort me. She is a very spiritual person, and her faith is unwavering. With that said she told me to pray, and to have faith that God will keep and protect me. There is power in words, and everything that she said to me resonated loud and clear. I don't know what I would do without this remarkable woman. My dad picked up the other phone and issued his own words of comfort, care and concern. What wonderful parents!

I headed home with nervous anticipation of what the next few weeks, and months would bring. What was wrong with me? Is it serious, life threatening or merely something very minor that could easily be fixed? I had phoned home to tell my husband about the events of the day, so he was eagerly awaiting my arrival. He had numerous questions, some of which I had answers and some not. I sat down, and delivered a brief explanation to Mareva. I did not want to alarm her so I simply told her that I had to have some routine tests performed. I quickly changed the subject and went about getting the girls ready for bed, and preparing myself for the next day.

I woke up thinking and believing that the previous day was all a dream. Was it true that something was terribly wrong with my heart, or was my mind simply playing tricks on me? Of course, after I gained my bearings I knew that it was all too real, so I proceeded to get dressed, take the kids to school, and drive to work.

I was only at work for about one hour, when I received a phone call from my doctor's office stating that I needed to call a cardiologist immediately, and make an appointment. The young lady on the line provided me with all the information as to whom I would be seeing. She also told me that they would run all of the normal tests to figure out what was going on inside my body.

Two days later I was sitting in the waiting room of the cardiologist who would oversee my care. I eagerly anticipated hearing my name called so that I could begin this journey. I heard my name, and followed the nurse into the tiny examination room. She took my vitals, and explained to me that I was having a couple of tests performed and what the tests entailed. I was an anxious candidate, so I told her that I was ready to begin.

I was hooked up to an EKG machine for a few minutes, and then escorted to another room which held an ultrasound machine. The nurse stepped out to notify the doctor that I was ready to proceed. The doctor entered and I was nervous with anticipation of what would be revealed. The doctor explained the procedure which he was about to perform and told me to relax. I guess he could see the angst on my face which let him know that I was terrified. The nurse asked me to hold out my right arm, and she injected me with a contrast dye that entered into my blood stream. She then spread a gel-like substance over my chest and handed the doctor a scope to use for the procedure. Almost immediately the doctor and nurse focused their eyes on the monitor, and silence had consumed the room. I felt helpless lying there because I wanted to see what they were seeing, and were in awe about. It was killing me.

They began talking to one another after a couple of minutes and then they proceeded to take pictures of what they were viewing. Ten minutes had elapsed, and the doctor informed me that he was finished. He exited the room while the nurse cleaned the gel from my chest. She asked me to get dressed, and advised me that she would return in a few minutes.

I was so very eager to find out what it was that they were so amazed about. I dressed myself in a flash, and waited for the door to open. I sat there for at least twenty minutes, and I could not imagine why it was taking so long. Finally, the nurse came to get me, and escorted me into the doctor's office. He came right to the point and told me that I had a rare heart condition that would require more tests. He also proceeded to tell me that he needed to consult with a cardiologist from Children's Hospital in Seattle, since he had never seen this type of defect in an adult, but had heard of children with the condition.

There was a cloud of mystery in my mind, and I blurted out, "What is wrong with my heart?" He said, "I am not sure, that's why we are going to perform additional tests." So, I then asked "What did you see on the ultrasound?" His reply is that the blood flow through the chambers of my heart was abnormal, that the route which the blood travels through the heart and lungs was different than what it should be. Well, was this a bad thing, was it life threatening? I knew that something would have to be done to correct this since I was running out of air after brief periods of exertion. The doctor told me that I could go, and that he would be in touch with me regarding what tests would follow.

Now, remember Lauren still needed to have hip surgery, so I was dealing with trying to figure out how on earth I would handle all that was on my plate. It was the fall, and Thanksgiving was right around the corner, so I thought that this would be a good time to schedule her procedure. I was able to take a leave of absence from my job, and my mom flew from Huntsville to Seattle to assist as well.

Lauren's surgery day came, and everything went according to plan. There were no complications with the procedure, and she was put in what is called a "spica" cast. The cast started a bit below her chest all the way down to her feet. She and I stayed at the hospital for about three days, and then we were sent home. I thought to my self, one surgery down, and maybe another one pending.

6

The First Revelations

Dealing with Lauren in that cast was difficult. The cast itself was thick and heavy, and the way that she was positioned in it was awkward. Diapering was the worst; it was very cumbersome and messy. However we made the best of it, and she learned how to cope with the extra weight on her body. She had always taken things in stride despite all of the difficulties which lie before her. She was my little trooper, and one of the reasons why I had to keep on going.

Since my mom was helping me care for Lauren, I was able to return to a somewhat normal routine. I took Mareva to school each day, ran errands, cleaned, cooked, etc … Mom sat with Lauren for the most part, and she would read stories to her as well as watch her favorite television shows with her.

One day I decided to clean the garage while mom and Lauren napped. This chore had been on my list for sometime. The garage wasn't that junkie, but it could stand some organization. I put away toys, cleaned out boxes, stored and stacked items, and arranged garden tools. I was almost finished when I noticed a doll standing beside the hot water heater. It was a life size doll that someone had given to Mareva a while ago. She never played with it, so I thought that it was time to get rid of it. I grabbed it to go into the throw away pile when I noticed a towel wrapped around an object.

I sat down the doll and picked up the towel, when suddenly three "unlabeled" video tapes fell out. "Why were there video tapes in the garage?" I thought. I was curious as to the content of the tapes, so I immediately went into the house, and headed to my bedroom. I turned on the television and VCR, and inserted one of the tapes. As I sat down on my bed the tape began to play, and an image of a person, a woman, appeared. I got up off the bed, and moved closer to the television screen to get a better view, when another image appeared, and it was the backside of a man. As my eyes moved closer to the screen the images became clear to me. The woman was one of my best friends, and the man was my husband. They were embracing and kissing, when I noticed that the setting of this encounter was my bedroom. The head and foot board of my bed was recognizable; the color of the comforter, and placement of furniture was unmistakable. Yeah, it was my bedroom alright.

I could not believe my eyes, how and when did all of this take place? They continued to kiss, and began fondling one another. This proceeded by the removal of clothing, more fondling, and then thrusting movements, moaning and groaning. I was in a state of shock, how could these two people who have meant so much to me carry on this way?

This woman had cared for my child, we spent time together going out to dinner, to the movies, shopping, etc … Our families often got together for dinners, birthday parties, barbecues, and other such celebrations. I had opened my home to her and her family. We confided in one another, and I trusted her implicitly.

I had never known my husband to cheat, so this was a total surprise, and something that I never thought I would have to deal with in my life. I was numb; truly in shock. I had always held him in such high regard; he was my knight in shining armor. He was everything to me!

As I sat there looking at the other tapes that I had yet to view, I felt as if my world had stopped rotating on its axis. I knew in my heart that things would never be the same, and that my relationship with my husband would be altered for the rest of our lives.

I continued watching the tape of my husband and friend having sex in my home, in my bedroom, and in my bed. When they finished they laid there holding each other, talking, and watching television. What an intrusion of privacy to have this woman in my bedroom, and bathroom, using my space. She walked through my home with such ease and delight it was sickening.

The tape ended, and I was compelled to continue to watch the other two tapes. The setting for the second tape was a hotel room. There stood a partially clad woman getting on a bed with anticipation and excitement in her eyes. Next, enters the nude rear end of a man standing in front of a camera beside the bed. The man began to speak, and it was the voice of my husband. By now I came to the realization that all of these tapes must be starring my husband, with different women as his supporting cast.

Her face came into view and I did not recognize her. Thank God that it was not another so-called friend! He turned toward the camera, and his entire front side was revealed. She came toward him, and began engaging in oral sex. This went on for several minutes until they both got into bed. They kissed and hugged, and eventually had sex. I sat there again in anguish watching the man that I love sharing what was suppose to be just for me with another woman.

My husband must have really liked this woman as she was on the tape again in another hotel room. This time she was lying in the bed, and it appeared that they had finished having sex since the sheets were halfway off of the bed, and tussled all about. She lay on the bed smiling and saying all the while "Come here baby, come here." Her image on screen became clearer as the camera moved in on her. She pulled the sheets off of her to reveal her naked white skin, and she began fondling her breast and vagina. The camera moved in for a closer shot as she completed this act of masturbation, all of which was caught on tape right before my eyes.

Her voice became soft and subdued as the camera sat still on the bed. All of a sudden I caught a glimpse of my husband's face, as he moved in on her body for a closer view. First the camera caught his face between her legs performing oral sex. The next thing I saw was his fingers moving in and out of her vagina. I was stunned to see what I was watching. I became sick to my stomach, and I also felt my heart pounding outside of my chest with anger and rage.

Once the second tape ended I quickly began to watch the third and final tape. The setting once again was my home, my bedroom, and my bed. I had no idea who this chick was but she was all over him like a dog in heat. By this time I was simply without feeling or care. How could I be so stupid to not know that all of this was going on under my nose? At that moment I felt like an idiot, one of those stupid wives, a lost woman. I was void of feeling for self. What was I going to do? How would I do whatever it was that I was going to do? So many emotions filled the space between my ears. I was mad as hell. I also felt sad, confused, desolate, crushed, and tormented. You name it, and I felt it! How could he shatter my world like this? What did I ever do in life to reap what was raining down on me at this point in time?

I had always been a good wife and mother. I had always been a good person who cared, and did for others. I had always looked for the best in people and given everyone the benefit of the doubt. I had never been a hell raiser, never been one to seek out trouble or confrontation. I did not have a foul mouth, never drank nor smoked, never hung out in the streets, or at the clubs. I was always the good girl … someone with a quiet spirit. In many ways I think that he perceived my "meekness" as a weakness, thus thinking that he could do whatever, whenever!

My parents had always taught me to be a nice and respectful young lady and to keep God first in my life. I did all of the things that they told me to do, so why was this happening to me? Oh, how this hurt!

After sitting there in silence for so long, I realized that the tape had ended, and the only sound coming out of the television was that annoying sound we call "snow." I got up and began to rewind the video tapes, one after another. I grabbed an empty purse out of my closet, and put the tapes inside. While I was doing this, I dialed my husband's work number. After greeting me with "Hello," I quickly replied, "I've seen your video tapes." He tried to act dumb by saying, "What tapes?" I responded by saying, "Your sick, freaky video tapes that you were hiding beside the hot water heater in the garage." Then there was silence, and even more silence. I don't think that either one of us knew exactly what to say, so we just sat there holding the phone. He asked if we could discuss it when he came home from work, and I said, "Yes, we will talk about this today, make no mistake." We hung up the phone and there I sat motionless. I did not know what to do next; I was paralyzed at that moment in time.

Mother was calling my name, so I snapped out of it. She needed some assistance with changing Lauren. As soon as I walked up the stairs she took one look at me, and said, "What's wrong?" It must have been written all over my face. Was I that obvious? Was I that transparent? How could she tell that I was hurting? Our eyes met as I walked closer to her, and I embraced her in the manner which I had when I was a young child, hurt from an injury and seeking comfort. I began to sob uncontrollably and just hung on to her for dear life. After wetting her blouse with my tears, my mouth opened, and I revealed to her what it was that caused me so much anguish. I gave her a blow by blow description until she said, "Stop, I don't want to hear anymore." She just looked at me and said, "I am so sorry." She repeated this phrase over and over again. It would soon become my motto.

She sat me down and told me that if the girls and I wanted to leave, she would make the necessary arrangements for all of us to fly home to Alabama. She continued to say that infidelity was a form of abuse, and that I did not have to sit there and take it; I had options. I could tell that she was very, very angry, but she wanted me to make my own decision. As always, I thought of the girls first, so I told her that I needed to stay and talk to Marcus. I had to hear whatever it was that would spew from his lips.

I dried my eyes, and went back to my room to gather myself before picking Mareva up from school. I decided to phone my "so called" friend who had crossed the line by sleeping with my husband. After numerous attempts and several busy signals she answered the phone. She knew it was me from the caller ID, so she began by telling me how sorry she was about everything. I thought, "How did she know what I was calling her about?" It seemed my husband had called her to warn her that the "jig" was up. I told her to be quiet, to let me talk, and then I let her have it. I did not use profanity, and I did not get ugly. I just told her what was on my mind and in my heart. I spoke of the betrayal, the broken trust, and the sisterhood that I thought we shared that would now be nothing but a distant memory. I asked her if she hated me so much that she would cross the line of friendship for self gratification. I also asked her if it was worth what was coming down on her right now, if she had any remorse for her actions. I continued by telling her that she needed to tell her husband, and that I was not going to be the only one who suffered from this "bullshit." I gave her an ultimatum: if she did not come forward about her "dirty" deeds, then I would, and I remember giving her three days in which to do it. I tried to conclude the conversation by telling her that she no longer existed to me, and to never call me or contact me again!

Of course she insisted that I listen to her as she apologized profusely, and admitted to being with him only "twice." I thought to my self, "Oh, this was not the first time." Were they having an affair right under my nose? When did it begin? Had she been in my bed before? I suppose the joke was on me; they had pulled the wool over my eyes. What a pair! Her rhetoric continued with her expressing a desire to remain friends. I laughed, and hung up the phone with the feeling of both sadness and delight.

Three days had passed, and I made a phone call to her husband. I gave him a full accounting of his wife's dirty deeds and offered up the video tape as evidence. He said that he believed me, and did not want to see his beloved wife in such a negative light. Lucky for him as these images were not burned into his memory as they are mine, and will be forever.

7

My Open Heart to Surgery

What do I do with all of the information that is at my fingertips, at my disposal? Do I stay, do I leave? Do I still love him, hate him? I honestly could not answer these questions. I was so damned confused. What would I say to him when he came home, would he even be remorseful, would he apologize for his actions? I had no answers to any of these questions, my mind was blank.

I thought back for a moment on how I could possibly have missed the signs. I mean surely there were signs; you always have an intuition or a gut feeling about things. Most of the time women know, we just don't want to accept the truth which had my name written all over it. Suddenly things came back to me like recalling pieces of a dream. One night he went out drinking with his friends which was nothing out of the ordinary, but this time he came home really late, I think around 4a.m. I waited for him downstairs, and was stunned by his appearance as he walked through the door. He was reeking with the smell of alcohol, staggering, and stumbling about, and his pants were unzipped. He looked a mess! I questioned him as to his whereabouts and his activities, but he simply kept walking upstairs toward the bedroom. He never offered an explanation, and after futile attempts at making him talk, I decided to give up.

There was also another occasion when I found an opened condom wrapper in the car. I pressed him for an explanation, and the lame one that I received was that it belonged to his friend. Now I know that I am pretty naïve, but I would never call myself stupid and that is exactly what he must have thought of me. I didn't accuse him of anything, but I kept a watchful eye over things. I suppose my stupidity was the fact that I never thought that he would cheat, that he was happy, and that he would never break one of God's commandments.

Mother wanted me to pack my bags and bring the girls back to Alabama with her, but I was neither ready nor willing to give up on my marriage just yet. I still loved him, and our family. Thus, I had decided to stay and weather the storm, and try to work things out. Since I was a young girl all I ever wanted or dreamed of was having a family of my own. I began collecting items for a hope chest when I was fourteen years of age. I was never desirous of having fame and fortune, or working a high profile job. I simply wanted a loving and devoted husband, as well as children who would fill my world with joy and laughter.

He came home that evening with a subdued look on his face not knowing what I would say or do. We took a drive, and I remember being the only one talking. I asked him repeatedly about his actions, and why he did it. He could not even look at me, and his only reply was, "I don't know." Every question of mine garnered the same answer, "I don't know." Boy, I was frustrated beyond belief. I felt like shaking him so he would talk to me, but he never opened up. He wasn't remorseful, and was never very apologetic. Sure, he said, "I'm sorry," but that was all that I got from someone who just ripped my heart open wide. Again, did he hate me that much, that he would bring all of these women into our lives? He wouldn't even stand up like a man and truly admit his wrong doing? He admitted that he wanted us to remain a family and said that he would do whatever it took for this to happen. So, I took him at his word and forgave him.

As time passed, I found myself trying to prove to him that I was as desirable as the women on the tapes. I tried to dress, look and act the part. I wanted to mimic all of the events from the tapes, to re-enact each and every one of them. I did all of the things to him that they did. I humiliated myself! Yes, he was my husband, and we were in the confines of our bedroom, but I had never been very sexual. I grew up thinking that you should lose your virginity to your husband, and that you should not be promiscuous. With all that said, I was not very experienced at all, and sometimes I thought that this was the reason why he cheated. I was willing to learn, but maybe that would not be enough.

Lauren returned to school after recovering from surgery, and I returned to work after taking the leave of absence to care for her. Things were slowly getting back to normal. It was Christmas time so the girls were happy and life was good. My wedding anniversary was three days after Christmas, on December 28th. That year I was surprised with a diamond anniversary ring. I guess my husband was trying to make up for all of the heartache and pain that he had caused. And of course, being my gullible and insecure self, I received it with honor and pride.

The holiday season came and went without much fanfare. We seemed to be happy, and it appeared that we had weathered the storm. However, I was still under the care of a cardiologist trying to determine what type of heart problem I was experiencing.

The procedures and tests that I had endured were an Echocardiogram, Electrocardiogram and Cardiac Catheterization. I received a call around mid-January on a Thursday evening. My cardiologist came right to the point by saying that it was discovered that I had a rare congenital heart defect that would require surgery. My immediate response was, "What kind of surgery?" and he replied, "Open heart surgery." I was dazed at the mere suggestion of having this type of operation. He proceeded to give me the name and phone number of the cardio-thoracic surgeon that he would refer me to. Before concluding our phone conversation, he asked me if I had any questions, and I followed by saying, "Yes." I asked, "What exactly is a congenital heart defect?" His reply was that I have a heart defect, or imperfection that has existed from the time that I was born. He continued to explain that he had consulted a pediatric cardiologist who had only seen this type of defect in infants. The defect was rare and had only been detected in a few cases.

I hung up the phone with an assortment of feelings encompassing me. First, I was relieved that I now had a diagnosis for what I had been experiencing for months. Secondly, I was petrified at the thought of having my chest opened up and my heart worked on, similar to that of an eighth grade biology class dissecting a frog. But lastly, I was thankful to God for allowing me to live all of these years with an imperfect heart. At that moment I felt blessed, and for the first time a strong sense of purpose for my life.

A couple of weeks passed and I met with the surgeon. He explained to me that I was not getting enough oxygenated blood in the left side of my heart. A procedure would have to be done to open a passage, and allow for proper blood flow to this area of the heart. He went on to explain that I ran the risk of developing a blood clot, which could lead to a stroke that could further lead to paralysis or even death if I did not proceed with the surgery.

I listened very intently and openly. I also hung onto every word that he uttered. The surgeon explained in detail the procedure of open heart surgery, the risks and the recovery. He also gave me a blow by blow description of what he would do to my heart once he opened my chest cavity. Open heart surgery requires that the rib cage by sawed open, and spread in order to reach the heart. Once inside you are placed on a by-pass machine, which allows blood to continue to flow through the body while the heart is worked on. He continued by telling me that I would have a permanent scar on my chest of about five inches in length. It would take approximately two months to reach full recovery.

I was ready to do this, so I made an appointment to have the procedure performed one week later. This would allow me time to arrange for my mom to come back out to care for the girls. Mom was the best; she had always been there whenever I needed her, first with Lauren's birth, her surgery and now me. She was my true source of inspiration. It did not matter that I would be out of commission for two months; she simply wanted to help and to do whatever needed to be done.

Surgery day came and all went well. I was able to come home after a four day hospital stay. Once I was home, mom took great care of me and made sure that I was getting enough nourishment and rest. However, I gradually began to feel a heaviness in my chest that worsened as the days went by. It felt as if bricks were being stacked on me one by one. It hurt to lie down, and my breathing became labored. I not only had the long incision going down the center of my chest, but there was a smaller one just below it. Fluid began to ooze out of this incision which freaked me out!

My doctor's office said that it was nothing to worry about, but to call back should it continue. The next day I woke up unable to breathe. My chest felt like a water soaked sponge. If you pressed down it would contract and expand. Mom immediately took me to the emergency room where the doctors tried to regulate my breathing. I was admitted to the hospital since I was having post operative complications. After numerous tests, it was discovered that I developed a staph infection. So now, what exactly is staph, and how do you get rid of it? Staphylococcus is a bacterium which forms in clusters or chains which causes pus to form in the body tissue. I had a chest full of this stuff!

The surgeon on call at the hospital that evening explained all of this to me. He also informed me that he would have to open up my chest cavity once again. I headed back to surgery not knowing what to expect this time around, but I was relieved that the infection was discovered. I woke up with two tubes protruding from my chest. I asked the nurse how my surgery went, and she simply answered, "Well." She continued to say that the doctor would be in to explain everything to me. As I waited, I became more conscious of my surroundings and caught my bearings. The doctor arrived, and told me that I had a very serious infection. He continued to tell me that I had a large amount of fluid sitting on my chest. He had to irrigate the area very well before stitching my chest up once again. I was also told that I would have to remain in the hospital until the infection had cleared, and that I would need to remain on antibiotics for at least a couple of months. As a result of the infection, I would need to have my chest irrigated every three hours. The irrigation was a process by which medicated fluid was inserted into my body through the tubes in my chest, and then flushed back out. I was also required to take antibiotics intravenously, which lasted for the duration of my hospital stay and beyond.

Halfway into what turned into a two week sojourn, I experienced midnight calamity. Two nurses, whom had never irrigated my chest, entered my room to perform the procedure. They looked confused as to what they should do, and how they should do it. I explained to them the five "w's" (who, what, where, when and why). They proceeded with much hesitation and confusion. They were almost finished when I began to feel heavy pressure in my chest, and my breathing became shallow. I asked them to stop and draw out the fluid, but they kept pushing more of the solution into my body. Suddenly, one of them realized that they had inserted too much into my system, and they began frantically to draw it back out. I was in a lot of pain and just upset from this entire ordeal. My sister Cathy had put her life on hold to come stay with me in the hospital. She was an eyewitness to this mass confusion, and tried to calm me down.

Cat, as we affectionately refer to her, is about a year and a half older than me. She is a wonderful person with a great big heart. Cat is deeply spiritual, and has a strong sense of self and family. When she found out that I had a serious infection she dropped everything including work, and school, and flew from Georgia to be with me. She stayed there in the hospital with me day in and day out. She only went home to shower and change clothes.

On that particular night she called Marcus, since I was so upset over the ordeal with the nurses. It was about three o'clock in the morning, and he was no where to be found. Mother was at home with the girls so she answered the phone. She went to get him but said that he was not home. I was livid, and of course, thought the worst. How could he be out on the town while I am in that hospital in misery? I immediately thought "Where was he, and who was he with at 3 o'clock in the morning?" I remember crying, and was really sad and upset. Cat tried to calm me down once more, but I did not want to hear it. How could he do this to me? How?

Later that morning my breathing was very erratic. The nurse came in, and asked what was wrong since all of my vitals were being monitored at the nurse's station. I explained that it was difficult to catch a breath. She left, but immediately returned to tell me that I was experiencing an abnormal arrhythmia. In other words, my heart was off of its normal rhythm. She further informed me that it was necessary to shock my heart back to its normal rhythm. The doctor brought in a crash cart, paddles and all; he then began the procedure. After all of this flurry of activity, the doctor asked me about the events of the previous evening. He told me that it was imperative for me not to get upset about anything, since it would impede my healing and recovery. I took his words to heart, and one week later on my birthday, February 21st, I was released and sent home.

8

Southward Bound

My recovery went well, but anyone who has had open heart surgery will tell you that it is slow at best. I was sent home with the IV still in my arm, because I needed to continue the antibiotic treatment for six additional weeks. I also could not pick up or lift any heavy objects, so Mother remained in Seattle for the two-month duration to take care of Lauren.

I was finally able to resume my life and return to work. I changed jobs and was now working with my good friend Theresa at another mortgage company. Theresa knew how busy and hectic my life was, so she knew that working at M&T Mortgage Corporation would be perfect. I held the position of senior loan officer and it afforded flexibility in my daily schedule. The drive to work was a bit longer than I was accustomed to but you learn to do what you have to do.

Work was going well, the girls were happy, and my husband and I were working things out. I was skeptical in thinking that things would ever be the same, but I had to give it a try. I could not give up on my family because this is all that I had ever wanted. I still loved him very much, and I just thought that people make mistakes. He insisted that he wanted our marriage to work and I believed him. However, with that said, every time he left our home I had a sinking feeling that he was still being unfaithful. I had no proof, it was just my intuition. I felt that I needed to put the past behind me if I were to truly give my marriage another chance. So, I decided to destroy the video tapes that had been holding me hostage. My husband and I destroyed them together and made a pact to renew our love for one another.

My prayers were answered when my husband was offered a job down South, in Marietta, Georgia. Marietta is a suburb of Atlanta, and more importantly only a three hour drive from my family and hometown of Huntsville, Alabama. I was ecstatic to be going home and to once again be close to my parents and siblings. My husband left in February of 2002 and the girls and I would wait until school was out in June to join him. I really didn't look forward to yet another separation, but I had prayed that this would be the last. So off he went.

I immersed myself in my job and the girls. Having to do everything myself was difficult. I felt like a single parent. My friend Kim was a really big help. She picked Lauren up from daycare and took her to school for me three days out of the week. Lauren spent her mornings at daycare and her afternoons at school, so I would have to leave my job, which was 30 miles one way to take her to school. I often used my lunch break to accomplish this task, which sometimes took up to an hour and a half depending on traffic. I would also have to be back at the school in the middle of the afternoon or a specific time to pick-up both Lauren and Mareva. Having help was a true blessing, one which I was thankful to receive.

I could always count on Kim. I sincerely felt that she was a true and life-long friend. I wanted to confide in her about recent events in my life, but I was too ashamed, and did not want her to judge me. I felt close to her, and knew in my heart that she was someone who would always be in my life.

Mother came to my rescue once again as she cared for Lauren while I packed up our house to prepare for the move. It was a difficult task, but one in which I embraced with enthusiasm. Marcus returned to put the boxes and furniture in storage. Kim took the girls and me to the airport. While I was sad to say goodbye to so many wonderful friends it was nice to be leaving this place that would remind me of heartache and pain. I just knew that moving to Georgia would be a fresh beginning for my family and me.

Marcus had been staying with his friend Tony, so now it was time to find a house for the family. Well we finally found a house and settled in Marietta. My husband had a really good job, therefore we both thought it best that I be a stay-at-home mom. This decision was not made lightly. We both knew that Lauren would require a lot of time and attention. We would have to locate services for physical, occupational, and speech therapy. We would also need to find a school with a good quality special education program. At that time she was of kindergarten age, and spent most of her days in a traditional school setting. Most importantly, finding doctors for her would also be a challenge. Lauren had been under the care of a neurologist as well as an orthopedist. All of this would take time, so not having to work was a blessing.

I truly believe that everything happens for a reason, and that there is no happenstance in life. I found a good team of physicians to care for Lauren's needs, so I was pretty comfortable with anything that may occur. Lauren started to stare into space, which was then followed by jerking movements of her entire body. These events sometimes lasted for a few seconds, but could continue for up to a couple of minutes. At first, I was scared and confused by her behavior until it became repetitious. Nothing seemed to trigger this activity; it would just happen out of the blue. One day she kept having these episodes, so we rushed her to an urgent care facility. I described what was happening to Lauren to the doctor on-call and upon examining her; he suggested that she was suffering from a type of seizure disorder.

Of course, I had read that there was a connection between cerebral palsy and seizures because of the connectivity to brain activity. But what I didn't know was if this would be something that would go away, or would it be a lifelong disorder. Lauren would soon undergo a series of tests that included an MRI and CT scan once more. The neurologist did in fact come back with a diagnosis of Lauren having general seizures which affect the entire body. With medication her seizures would become manageable, but none the less frightening to witness. I hated that fact that my baby had to endure what appeared to be "pain" piercing through her body. Sometimes she would fall off to sleep after an episode.

After trying a couple of different seizure control medications, the seizures occurred on a weekly basis instead of daily. Whenever Lauren became ill, constipated, or really tired I knew that a seizure would soon ensue. There was no way of knowing if the seizures would ever cease, however, what I did know was that I had to do all that I could to ensure that she had the very best in care.

Since we only lived three hours from my hometown it was a blessing to be able to see my family more than once, or twice a year which was the case while we were living in Seattle. My family is a close-knit group, and if one person is in need, then the family rallied to that person's aid. We celebrated everything and we never went more than a couple of days without talking or emailing one another.

My girls are the only grandchildren that my parents have and the love that Joe and Shirley displayed to these kids was huge. I have two sisters Beverly and Cathy, and one brother, Joe, Jr. All of my siblings are special in their own unique way. Beverly's the oldest and she is the leader of the pack. She is always on top of things and in total control. Beverly's a Janet Jackson look-a-like and a true big sister in every possible way. My sister Cathy is the salt of the earth. She is so kind and free hearted. She is also very spiritual with deep rooted beliefs. Cat sports a short sleek hair style and is a brown eyed beauty. She lives in Union City, a suburb south of Atlanta. It was wonderful having my sister so close to me, thank you God! My brother Joe Jr., who was next to me in age and the youngest, is a free spirit. He has had trouble with substance abuse for most of his life and was desperately trying to get it together. He is a handsome young man who has worked as a personal trainer for years. His struggle is great, but with the love of his family, and faith in the almighty he will one day find peace.

9

Déjà Vu: Here we go again

It was three o'clock in the morning, and Marcus was not home. He went out with his friend Tony, whom he lived with upon his arrival to Georgia. I waited up for him because I was worried. It was getting really late. He came in, seemingly under the influence of alcohol, and dared me to question his whereabouts. We had a brief discussion, but I got nowhere. I felt as if he were hiding something from me. It was déjà vu all over again.

The next morning after getting the girls off to school, I had that feeling again that something was just not right. I looked in our room, specifically our closet, for answers. I found a cell phone bill. There were pages and pages of phone numbers. So, I began to call the numbers. Now mind you, there were a few numbers on the bill that he had called several times. One number especially stood out, not just because it was a Canadian number, but because he had called this number nearly every other day.

I dialed the number, and it just rang. After the forth ring a woman's voice spoke out via voice mail. She stated her name, which I no longer can recall, and her voice brought a personality to these phone numbers. After the beep, I left her a message that my husband had been calling her for some time, and that I wanted to know why. I politely asked her to call me back as soon as possible, and then I hung up the phone.

I examined the bill highlighting all of the numbers that did not ring a bell. I dialed each and every one. Each number brought forth the voice of a woman leaving her personal greeting. Who were these women and what was going on? Most of the calls were from Seattle and surrounding cities area codes. Where would this paper trail lead me? I left messages stating that their phone number appears on my husband's cell phone bill numerous times, and that I wanted to find out who they were and what sort of relationship they had with him.

One of the women actually returned my call. It was the woman behind the Canadian number that my husband so frequently called. She began by asking me that if she told me everything, would I please not call her again. I replied, "Yes," and this is what she had to say: she met my husband over a year ago in Seattle, and had been seeing him ever since. Their relationship, she contended, began as a friendship which became sexual in nature. He had been to Canada to see her; she had been to Seattle to see him. He had sent her a plane ticket to meet him in Las Vegas for a weekend. He had also sent her a plane ticket to visit him in Atlanta, after he moved to begin working his new job. While here in Atlanta they stayed at a swank hotel in the downtown area and he wined and dined her for what she explained was a "magical" weekend.

She continued to say that he had told her that we were separated, and were in the process of getting a divorce. Wow, this was news to me! The very day that the girls and I left Seattle, he had her in his bed after taking her to dinner.

After her dissertation, I kindly informed her that he and I were still together, and that we had never discussed a separation or divorce. She had been under the impression that I was living in Alabama with my parents, so when I told her otherwise she became agitated and uttered the words "typical black man." I asked her what she meant by her comment, and she said that the father of her son was a black man and that all he did was lie about this and that. She revealed to me that she was Caucasian, and had negative experiences with black men. So, tell me why was she messing around with my husband for all of this time if she felt this way?

She expressed the fact that she was upset by my phone call because he was so nice and kind to her, and she had thought that they were developing a serious relationship. The nerve of her being upset, what about me? I am the last to know about this relationship, but isn't that how it goes, the wife is the last to know?

This woman, supposedly, was going to call or email him to give him a piece of her mind. She assured me that she would not contact or see him again. Did I really care? Did she think I really wanted to know? I couldn't be upset with her, but I was mad at the situation. I appreciated all of her candor and honesty, and am glad that she "fessed up" to the affair. I just thought to myself, "Here we go again!"

This man was living a double life. All the while I was thinking that he was this wonderful, dedicated, and devoted husband, who had learned from his past mistakes. But instead he is out in the world playing Casanova to another woman. I was pissed that I had allowed this to happen to me again. Were there signs that I missed or simply did not want to see? Was my past coming back to haunt me? Was I in denial? Had my head been in the sand? How could I possibly be in this situation yet again?

While I realize that he was working out of town, and only saw his family once every two months, I had still tried to give him the benefit of the doubt and to trust him again. Wasn't that the right thing to do? I had tried to salvage our marriage, but now it may be too late.

I remember hanging up the phone and sitting on the floor in the middle of my closet just crying my heart out. I felt so empty. I felt dirty and ashamed like I had been used up. I was in so much agony that I can still feel the pain and the emptiness that it brings. I just wanted to run away and hide. I was mad and really upset with myself.

I got up after sitting there for an hour. I needed some kind of confirmation to the story told to me by this stranger who had entered my life. I needed validation. She had told me that my husband's friend, Tony, knew of their affair. She also mentioned that he had accompanied them on the trip to Las Vegas. She had even brought along a friend to meet Tony.

So, I called Tony to get the "411" on all of this mess that I now had to deal with. After a long and hurtful conversation, everything that she had told me was corroborated. Tony apologized for his part in Marcus's deception and said that he had wanted to tell me what was going on for quite some time, but couldn't because of his friendship with my husband. He continued on to tell me that he considered me his friend as well, and didn't condone what Marcus had done. I asked him why he was so forthcoming about this information, and he replied that he no longer cared about his friendship with my husband, and that I didn't deserve to be treated in this manner. He offered his shoulder to lean and cry on, but I never once thought of "payback." I am a firm believer in two wrongs do not make it right, so I was not walking down that path.

I hung up the phone, and continued searching to find anything else that he was hiding. I was so fed up with the lies, deceit, betrayal, and intrusion of these women into my life. Midway into my search I discovered a roll of film that hadn't been developed. So, I got in my car, and dropped off the film for one hour processing. When I picked up the film, I was very reluctant to open the package and view its contents. I recognized some of the people as my husband's friends from Wichita, Kansas, where he had previously worked. I did not, however, recognize the woman who was sitting on my husband's lap, and in other compromising positions.

Had he had yet another affair? How many more women were out there, and how many more would I find out about? What did I ever do to him? I kept asking myself "Why?" The revelation of Marcus's deceit brought about feelings that I had never thought that I would experience. I had been on the verge of believing in him and trusting in his love for me once again when all of this happened. Maybe God was trying to tell me something, as the song goes; maybe it was time to get out.

I desperately wanted and needed to talk to someone, I needed advice and direction. I remember calling my sister, Cathy, and pouring out everything I had learned. Her response was that I always had a home, or a place to stay since she only lived about 30 minutes from me. She did not tell me what to do, but she did empathize with my situation. She asked me if I wanted to seek counseling, and offered her church pastor as someone to confide in. I told her that I would think about it and be in touch. She is the only family member that I spoke of these recent events to because I knew that my mom, dad and sister Beverly would have been furious. They would have come to Georgia and packed my bags themselves. I just needed some time to think.

I continued with my day, picked up the girls from school, cooked dinner, etc … He called before coming home. His "mistress" had emailed notifying him that he had been "busted!" Since he had been out the night before and had tied one on he asked me if he could take a nap before I began yelling at him. This statement told me that he did not care at all about me or my feelings. I guess I was nobody to him: insignificant, useless, and just someone to call his wife, and to take care of the children. He arrived home and sure enough went upstairs to nap. I did not yell, make a scene, or appear to be upset, since I did not want the girls to feel the affects of his wrongdoing.

I was able to speak to him that evening, and of course my main question was, "Why", and, "How on earth could you do this to me again?" His only reply was, "I don't know, I guess lack of discipline." I simply could not believe my ears. He was not sorry or remorseful; he just chalked it up to one of those things that just happened. At that point my marriage was in deep, deep trouble. I didn't feel there was any way out. So should I simply stay for my children? I no longer felt the love and passion that I once felt for him. I no longer yearned for his touch, his kiss, or his embrace. He had given that to all the other women that he was with, and nothing was sacred unto our union as a couple anymore. He had brought all of these people into our lives, into our home and into my heart. I did not feel that a special type of love surrounded, and protected us as I thought it had in the past. It was all gone, just like that, poof!

Yet again after much thought, I decided to stay and tough it out. I purchased books for him; sought out, and did research on the internet for him; talked with him, etc … It was my belief that he was a sex addict who needed help. It is in my nature, and a big part of who I am to try and save or fix what is broken. I thought that it was incumbent upon me to help him get rid of these demons, to be there for him and to let him know that I still believed in him. I tried to convince myself of all of this, but did I sincerely believe it? Yeah, it sounds good to try to help or save someone, but you have to believe in the person or at least think that they will try to help themselves. I am such a proponent for the underdog and down trodden. So, for all of these reasons I decided to try to love him again, and to be all that he wanted and needed me to be. Again, I figured I had something to prove to him, to show him that I was some kind of wife, some kind of mother and some kind of lover. All of this sounded good, but would it really happen, would it work?

10

Masquerade

I think that I had missed my calling, and should have become an actress since I was putting on a show for everyone. I'd smile on the outside, but was dying on the inside. I no longer cared about "Pam", she was just this woman, who cooked, cleaned, and cared for her children. I began to go out of the house wearing sweat pants, tee shirts and tennis shoes every day of the week. I never did much to my hair, always pulled it back in a bun. I was frumpy; I had put on some weight and just didn't care. Again, I thought that I could not do any better, that this was the life that was meant for me. I never thought that anyone else would love me. My husband was never physically abusive, and he was a hard worker who provided shelter, food, and clothing for his family. But, is that enough? Is it ever okay to go through life just having someone to call your spouse, but not feeling what that person is suppose to mean to you? Did God intend for a marriage soured to continue to spoil? I would continue to ponder these questions for sometime.

    I had made up my mind that I was no longer in love with him, yet I still loved him. Maybe the feeling of being in love would come back to me in time. Maybe we could find our way back to one another. I suggested that we try marriage counseling, but he flat out refused. He did not feel that a stranger could explain his feelings and actions to him, and that no one could tell him what to do, or how to feel. I really pushed for counseling, but as usual, he was the "man," so he had the final say. Since he didn't want to work on us as a unit, I decided to work on myself. I listened to all of the self help guru's on television, and read their books trying to understand why I suddenly found myself in such a predicament. Nothing really helped and I found myself settling in the role that most women come to, and that is putting me last. I really didn't mind all that much because my girls were my world. I simply lost myself and my identity. I was just "Mom." I really didn't know any better, or I would have done better. I became totally submissive and accepted the way that I was being treated.

During this time I found a wonderful church to attend, and the girls and I joined and became faithful members. I had always been spiritual and known that prayer was the answer to all things. Liberty Hill Missionary Baptist Church was more that just a place to worship, it was home. It was so welcoming and inviting, and we fit right in with the congregation.

On our second visit to the church, I remember meeting a woman who also had a daughter with cerebral palsy, as well as another daughter who diligently cared for her sister. This was the mirror image of my girls and me. This woman was a few decades older than me, as well as her children from my girls. She provided me with a glimpse into the future, as well as guidance and wisdom beyond belief. It was so nice to relate to someone and to share similar feelings. This woman had a lot of grace and poise, and I aspired to be like her. God had led me to this place of worship, and knew that this woman would be an inspiration in my life.

I also met a wonderful group of women, who had formed a support group for mothers of children with special needs. We met once a month to share in the ups and downs of our children's lives. We also shared our tears, needs, hopes, and dreams for the future. These women became my friends, people that I could call on and count on. We all shared in the struggle. They empathized with me, and knew how it felt to have to get up several times throughout the course of the night to reposition our children. They knew how it felt to spend hours on the phone fighting with insurance companies in order to get basic equipment. They also knew what it felt like to juggle your schedule to allow time for doctor's appointments and therapy sessions. This was our life, this was God's plan for us, and these were our special little angels.

Months came and went, and I never complained about a thing. My girls were happy, so that's all I really cared about. I hit my fortieth birthday, and decided to get a physical since it had been years since my last. Everything was normal except for my weight. I tipped the scales at 163 pounds. The only time that I had ever weighed this much was during my pregnancies with the girls. I was in a total state of disbelief. I had always been a small framed person who never had to deal with weight issues. I was at least 25 pounds overweight. Since this was a new doctor we discussed my past medical history in depth. He was a bit concerned about these extra pounds, especially since I'd had past problems with my heart. He suggested that I begin an exercise regimen, as well as monitoring my food intake. According to my height of 5'7", my target weight should be no more than 145–150 pounds; therefore my doctor informed me that I should lose about 15 pounds.

I went home, and thought about my visit to the doctor. I used to exercise a lot, and had always been physically active. I had no desire to work on my body, my looks, or my attitude. Why did I have such low self esteem? I was mentally and physically in a rut! I sincerely thought in my heart that this would be my life for the rest of my life. I also thought, as I gazed in the mirror that no one would want to be with me with this scar on my chest, it was horrible. I also looked at the stretch marks from my child bearing years and now I had to contend with the extra pounds surrounding my hips and thighs. But the one thing that I knew for sure is that no one would ever want to be with me since I had a child with a disability.

Don't get me wrong, I love Lauren with every breath in my body, but I am trying to be realistic. I know how difficult it is to care for her, how time consuming and how daunting of a task. I did it without question or hesitation since she came from my flesh, from my blood, and from my body. But, I also knew that if I were single again that it would be almost impossible for anyone to be sincerely interested in me, knowing that I have a child with cerebral palsy. I did not want to be alone, so I settled for this broken marriage with love, faith and compassion long gone, and with little hope of ever retrieving it.

The next set of events would rock my foundation. The girls and I were on our way to school one Monday morning, as I always dropped them off instead of having them ride the bus. Mareva and I dropped Lauren off first, and then proceeded to her middle school. It was a bright, sunny fall morning, and traffic was steady as it always was this time of the day. I was less than a mile from her school when I looked in my rear view mirror, and noticed a truck approaching me at an unusually fast rate of speed. Traffic was stopped so I was just sitting there looking at the truck wondering if it were going to stop. I suddenly flung my right arm across Mareva's chest, and tried to brace us for the impact. The truck struck us with such force that we both jolted forward, as if we were riding on a roller coaster. The crash terrified Mareva into tears, and my first instinct was to check for injuries. Other than being in a state of confusion and shock, we were both alright and without any physical injuries.

A figure soon appeared at my door. I rolled my window down, and there stood a young man, just a kid, and he looked as if he were barely old enough to drive. He asked if we were okay, and I responded "yes." He then remarked that he would call the police to report the accident. I quickly regained my wits and composure, and was able to drive the car off to a side street. I got out of my car to survey the damage, and what I viewed was horrific! The entire trunk and back side was smashed in. It compared to the way a stepped on soda can looks. I was amazed that we were not hurt. The police soon arrived, as well as the young man's father. Well, it turned out that the driver was only sixteen years of age. He was cited with speeding, and reprimanded pretty harshly by the police officer for his reckless driving.

After driving this mangled and twisted up heap of metal home, I soon came to an astonishing revelation. What if Lauren had been in the car with us? Oh my God, what would have happened to her? She would have certainly been badly injured, because she always sits in the back seat. She has poor head and neck control, so there is no telling what would have happened to my baby girl. I transported her wheelchair in the trunk, so this would have been destroyed. The accident occurred approximately ten minutes after dropping her off at school. I began thanking God for sparing my child's life; it was by his grace that she was not in the car with us.

I have a network of family and friends that I email frequently, so as usual I sent out a testimony detailing the events of the day. I always like to tell of God's work in my life, as I feel that it gives people hope and inspiration to hear of God's never ending love. I also shared this story with members of my church at our Wednesday evening bible study class. I remember one woman coming up to me at the end of class. She was a respected, longtime member and mother of the church. She hugged me long and hard, and looked me in the eye and said, "God favors you." She repeated this phrase a couple of times, all the while holding my hand, and looking me in the eye. I just smiled at her not knowing exactly what she meant, so I nodded my head in agreement. She continued to tell me to keep God first in my life, and that he would always take care of me and my children.

My grandmother, Rosetta, often spoke of God blessing me for taking care of his child and creation. She also felt that not everyone could take care of a child with a disability, that I was "selected" and should consider it an honor and privilege. I must say that it hardly felt like an honor having to reposition Lauren's body at three o'clock in the morning night after night! Sometimes it's hard to see the wisdom that our parents and grandparents, or elders bestow upon us. My grandmother had been through a lot and experienced much in her life, so when she spoke I listened. She had always been someone that gave good and sound advice. She had also experienced some of the same issues of infidelity in her own marriage, so she knew of the pain and heartache. She knew how it felt to have your marriage corrupted and marred. She knew of lost faith, trust, and hope. She and my mom had always been my inspiration, my role models and my heroines.

Soon after the accident I received a call from my dear and close friend Marla, who lives in Los Angeles. She said that she had read my email, and had to hear my voice. I've known Marla for over fifteen years. My husband and a previous boyfriend of hers had worked together in the Los Angeles area, and through their acquaintance, she and I met. We hit it off immediately, and had much in common. We shared February as our birth month, and would always celebrate with a nice bottle of champagne. She and I would periodically wear braids, and Marla hooked me up with a sista that could really braid hair. We would often go to get our hair "did" together, and would laugh and talk, and just have the best time in the world. Marla is a beautiful black woman who is fun loving, free spirited, kind, and real. I trust her implicitly, and she is a real confidante. I regard her as a sister, more than merely a friend. I love her, and can always count on her for anything that I need. Our friendship has sustained over the years, and I know that she is a lifelong friend.

Anyway, upon reading my email, and knowing of all of my trials and tribulations she came up with a suggestion. She said to me, "You should write a book." It is ironic that she would say this; I had also been thinking about the same thing.

I suppose the reason I would share my testimonies was to reach out and help someone in need. I had been through a few things, and had experiences that others may not have had at such a young age, so I could speak to what I knew. Sharing life's ups and downs not only make us stronger, but wiser as well. You gain a perspective that you may never have thought that you are capable of possessing. You learn thus you grow.

11

Awakenings

The year was 2005 and like everyone else I made my New Year's resolutions. At the top of my list was to loose the extra pounds that I had accumulated. I received a gym membership as a Christmas present. This was really the only thing that I had asked for because I was determined to get fit. I began working out at the YMCA, which of course is geared toward family fitness. My first appointment was with a wellness coach who developed a program that would encompass cardio and weight training. I slowly began taking some aerobic classes as well. I thought to myself, "I feel great; I should have done this a long time ago!" I was finally doing something for myself, and it was exhilarating and wonderful.

I soon developed my own routine, and would workout in the morning after taking the girls to school. Little by little the pounds began to shed, and I felt like I was taking control of my life again. Just prior to beginning my workout regimen, I'd had what I call a couple of "episodes" with my heart. I was at my parents' home in Alabama, and late one evening I went downstairs to retrieve a bottle of water. Returning up the stairs, I became disoriented. I sat down on the bed, and my ears began to ring. The television was on, but all I could see were lips moving; there was no sound. I could not hear anything except for that darn ringing. Soon thereafter I broke out in a cold sweat, and my heart felt like it was beating out of my chest. Suddenly, my heart seemed to stop beating. This lasted for about three minutes, and it totally freaked me out. I didn't know what to make of it. I did not tell anyone because I thought that it was a rare anomaly, and would not happen again. The symptoms repeated themselves the very next morning, but this time I fell and hit my head. It felt as if I was having a heart attack. My parents were terrified, and urged me to seek help immediately upon my return home. My physician referred me to a cardiologist, and due to my past heart issues, I was subjected to the normal litany of tests. Every test came back negative, and I was told that it was stress and anxiety that had caused these episodes.

I tried to take it easy, and not get upset over things that I had no control over, but my life is just stressful. Taking care of a child with a disability was just hard, and it was a daily struggle. Lauren was totally dependent upon me for every aspect of her life, not to mention the fact of her seizure disorder, and the numerous doctors' appointments. All of this made it very difficult to get any relief. Mareva was also a handful participating in many activities. She played sports as well as a musical instrument, so we were always on the go. There was also the fact that I was trying to regain trust in my marriage, but every time the phone rang and no one said anything, I would think that he was still cheating. I had no proof, but often history has a way of repeating itself over and over again.

I had to start thinking of myself, my health, and my wellbeing. I again re-examined my life, and my feelings. At this point my heart was just hardened, and I felt that I was merely here for the sake of my children. I began to feel like there was no hope, and that it was over. We had serious issues in the bedroom and I had, for the very first time, thought that it may be time to end my marriage. We no longer connected as a couple, we no longer shared the same interests, and we were spiritually disconnected. The passion and desire no longer existed between us. As hard as I tried, I had lost all respect for this man that I had known and loved for half of my life. In the past, I regarded him as my knight in shining armor, my soul mate, my life partner, and my best friend. I no longer saw him as any of these things. The wounds are deep and divided. My heart was not just broken, it was shredded into pieces. My lifetime dream of being in love, and being loved by a wonderful man was nothing but a memory. It's all gone, all of it!

So what was holding, or keeping me here for so many years? Fear, I suppose. I figured out that it is always difficult to "step out" of your comfort zone. I did not want to be the one who caused my family to crumble, to split, and to separate. But after much thought and prayer, I came to the conclusion that it wasn't me. He was the one who was not content, not prayerful, and not hopeful of change. He was the one who stepped out on our commitment to one another, time after time, again and again. This was not my burden to carry, or my cross to bear. Nothing had changed between us; nothing was different, or renewed. If this man loved me like he claimed, wouldn't he have gone to the ends of the earth to try and change the climate of our marriage? It was time for me to "step out" on faith, to regain myself, to find that woman who had been lost and forgotten. It was time to love me again!

I vividly remember receiving a phone call from my oldest sister Beverly, asking me how I wanted to celebrate my wedding anniversary that year. The call came in July, as she wanted ample time to plan in the event that I wanted something elaborate for a milestone year. You see my 20th wedding anniversary would take place on December 28th. I was speechless as she waited for my reply. I don't know why nothing came out of my mouth; I had always wanted to renew our vows. I felt like we needed to start anew, to re-fresh our commitment to one another, and to God. In the past I had suggested all of this to my husband, but he was never interested so I forgot about it, and lived with another disappointment. I told my sister that I would think about it, and get back to her. I spent the next two months pondering her question. Something was stirring inside my soul.

My mom had once told me that no one could tell me when to leave my marriage, or to leave it at all, but that I would know in my heart and soul when I had enough and was ready to leave. My mind began to rewind the passage of time. I went back over 23 years to the beginning when we first met, to the good times, and to the bad. I had a secret that I had kept all of this time. It weighed heavily on my mind. Marcus had proposed to me over the phone, which was common knowledge. He was in the Marine Corps stationed quite a distance away from our home town of Huntsville. We had dated for approximately three years, but had spent the last year apart. We had our issues but always seemed to find our way back to each other. After his proposal he was hesitant about speaking any further. I answered by saying, "Yes, I will marry you", and he became silent. I asked what was wrong, and he told me that he had something to tell me. I listened intently, and he said that a woman in the Marine Corps, who was stationed at his base, may be pregnant with his child. Suddenly, the cat had my tongue. After a minute or two I asked, "Is it yours?" His reply was, "I don't know, maybe." He went on to tell me that he had only slept with this woman twice, and that he was no longer involved with her. Well, it only takes one sexual encounter to get pregnant, so he may be that child's father.

I told him that it didn't matter, and that we could work it out. What was I thinking? What was I doing? What was wrong with me? When I look back on these events I have to wonder if God was trying to give me a sign. Was I that desperate that I would forge ahead to make such a commitment, without talking or consulting with anyone, not even my mom? Stupidity is a by-product of youth and boy was I "dumb" when it came to affairs of the heart. I blocked this from my mind like it never occurred and walked down that aisle with problems already in the making. I set myself up from day one, the hurt and pain had already begun. All I wanted was a husband, to be married, wear the white dress, walk down the aisle, and show off my ring. Why did I not know that this was not what holy matrimony was all about? How could I have been so blind and so careless with my life?

12

A Leap of Faith

Fall was in the air, and with the change of the season came the change that I would soon make in my life. After searching my soul, praying to the Almighty, and walking by faith, I decided to tell my husband that I wanted a divorce. I was no longer scared of what the future would hold for me. I was no longer scared of being alone, and thinking that no one would ever want to be with me because I had a child with a disability. I was no longer scared of feeling inadequate and inferior from being treated like a child. I no longer felt the depression and isolation that had consumed me for so very long. I was no longer scared of wondering how and where I would live since I did not have a job. Fear no longer gripped neither my soul nor my spirit. I was ready to face whatever God had in store for me, and I wanted to run on.

It was very difficult, but I sat my husband down, and after much discussion I told him that I wanted a divorce. He did not think that I was serious, and as usual took what I had to say for granted. I guess he thought that I was bluffing. I began to sleep in the guest room, and I started to think about my liberation. He kept trying to talk to me about my decision. He tried to get me to change my mind, but my mind had been made-up a while ago, and now I was finally doing something about it. My husband now wanted to try therapy or counseling. I could not believe it after all of these years, and numerous attempts of doing this in the past. I had no desire to salvage my marriage, for I no longer felt any kind of connection with this man I was once in love with. I no longer felt, or trusted that he would take care of me till death do us part. I just didn't feel special or loved by the one who agreed to love, honor, and cherish me on that day nearly twenty years ago. Maybe I believe too much in fairy tales, but I did not want to spend the rest of my life in a loveless marriage, especially since I am such a passionate and devoted person. Even if it meant being alone, I would still have the love of self, and that meant the world to me.

My husband finally accepted the inevitable, but refused to move out of the house. The tension was unimaginable, and it almost drove me crazy. It was very difficult trying to share space with someone whom you wish to cease communication with. He began to blame me for breaking up our home, and tried to lay a guilt trip on me regarding the girls. Lauren would not understand, but Mareva sure did. He thought that it would devastate her, but it didn't. In fact, a year prior to our break-up, she had suggested to me that her dad and I should separate and divorce. Children are very perceptive, and she noticed that we never kissed, never held hands, or showed affection to one another. She also noticed that he did not help out much at home, especially with Lauren. Mareva knew that I was sleeping in the guest room, and wanted to know why, so I provided her with a brief explanation. I told her that her dad and I were divorcing, and she said that she was glad, and that we should not stay together just because of her and Lauren. She continued to say that we both would be happier with other people.

I could not believe the wisdom and acceptance that came from my child's mouth, but after all she was a freshman in high school now, and had matured seemingly "overnight." I was so proud of her, and I made a vow that no matter what, her dad and I both loved her and her sister very much, and would always put that love first. I also told her that it was not her fault, nor Lauren's that we were divorcing, and that sometimes people grow apart from one another. I assured her of this over and over again, so that she knew it was a fact.

It was important that she be open and honest with me, since she was going through adolescence and this was a critical time in her life. She and I are extremely close, and can talk about any and everything. I had to feel in my heart that my child was okay with this recent set of events. I know her very well, and I always impressed upon her the value of being open and honest. Therefore, she opened up and shared her heart with me and everything was fine. Mareva confided that she had not felt that I was happy, that I always seemed depressed and down. She continued to say that I didn't enjoy life and that she felt as if she and her sister were a burden to me. She said that if I were happy then she and her sister would be happy as well.

Around this same time my dad had become ill. He had been in and out of the hospital battling the form of arthritis known as gout in his lower extremities. He had been plagued with asthma for as long as I can remember, and also had problems with his heart. My dad was one of a kind. I didn't really get to know him well until I was an adult and out of the house. I can forever remember him being a workaholic doing whatever he had to do to provide for his family. He not only worked outside the home, but he would do whatever needed to be done inside the home as well. He kept the kitchen floor sparkling clean, and did the same to the bathrooms. My dad also knew how to cook, and he picked up the slack whenever and wherever was needed. He was a very special person and a real family man. My girls are the only grandchildren that my parents have, so they showered them with much love and affection. Dad's eyes lit up whenever my girls were in his presence. He would get down to their level, and play with them. It was heart warming to see the three of them laugh, sing, dance and play.

Dad was also a cheerful giver. He did not care if you were black, purple, blue, green or white. Everyone was equal in his eyes. He often gave of his time, money or other possessions. Dad also believed in helping his neighbor. If anyone had any kind of need, be it large or small and he knew about it, he would try his best to help them in any way he could. He always put others first and never sought praise for helping out; it simply made him feel good.

Again, it's funny how things happen in our lives, and we call them "coincidences" when in fact, they are predestined. Well a person whom I had known for over twenty years re-entered my life. He and I had always been friends in college, and shared many of the same interests. We had shared a strong mutual attraction for one another back then, but never acted on it as the timing was not right. We saw each other at a party during Homecoming festivities at Alabama A&M University, the place where we had earned our degrees. It was as if time stood still. The feelings were prevalent even after all of this time. We talked, and I told him what I was going through, and he revealed to me that he had recently been through a divorce as well. He reminded me of my self worth, and told me to live each day to its fullest. My friend also conveyed to me the importance of showing your love for someone, and not just saying the words. He helped me to focus on the quality of my life, and the people who were in my life. My long lost friend would always call me "beautiful", and he would tell me that it radiated from the inside out. It had been such a long time since I heard these words from a man, especially one that I shared feelings with. I don't quite know what it was about him that made me believe that I was a beautiful and desirous woman, but I just thank God for our paths crossing once again. There is power in words and sometimes we all need to be reminded of things to make us feel good.

Another thing that helped me through this time was the fact that I started working again. I got a job as a Paraprofessional, a.k.a. teacher's aide, at the same school that Lauren attended, Kincaid Elementary School. I worked in a special education classroom which was comprised of children with varying disabilities. The children ranged in age from 8 to 11 years old with disorders such as Autism, Down Syndrome and Cerebral Palsy. It was great, and I fit in right off the bat. Having a child with special needs prepared me for this position, as I already possessed patience which is a "must" while working in the special education environment.

I was paired with a woman by the name of Francina. She is a very spiritual person who had previously experienced divorce herself. Again, God places people in our lives for specific reasons, and Francina helped me through some very dark days. She prayed with me and for me, she provided spiritual support in the midst of the chaos, and she truly cared about me. Francina is a beautiful woman of color who wore her natural hair with pride. I instantly knew that she was a good person with strong morals and values. We got along great from day one and I will forever value her friendship.

The girls and I went home to Alabama for Thanksgiving, but my husband decided to stay in Georgia. Most of my family, as customary, congregated at my parent's home for Thanksgiving dinner. We would always have a nice time for we loved to celebrate special occasions. You name it: birthdays, anniversaries, anything ... we would always find a reason to celebrate, just so we could get the family together. My family is of average size, which made it pretty easy for everyone to gather in one space. It was so nice being home with people who loved and cared for me, especially now. They all knew what was going on, and they provided the support that I needed.

It's not often that we make lasting memories, but this visit brought about some very special moments. My dad, Lauren, and I were home alone on the day after Thanksgiving. Dad had recently been released from the hospital, so he was taking it easy and not doing too much. I was washing dishes, upset about a phone call that my husband had made to my mom. My dad listened to me vent and cry. He really understood where I was coming from. He told me that while he hated that my long-running marriage was coming to an end that I needed to do what was best for me. He encouraged me to be strong and not look back. He understood that I would never be able to forget about those video tapes, and that I would carry them in my mind for the rest of my life. He did not want that for me and made it clear that he supported me and my decision 100%. Dad and I enjoyed the best conversation that I can ever remember because he had never talked a lot, and was a bit shy. He comforted me with his gentle touch, and he eased my soul with the love that only a father can provide. I was truly touched, and this will always hold a special place in my heart.

13

Dad's Home Going

January 12, 2006, was the day that my dad passed. I was in total and absolute shock when my sister Cathy called me at work with the news. How could this be true? Dad had been ill but it was not life threatening, so how did this happen? We did not get a chance to prepare, to say good bye, or to hug. Why? The day prior to his death had been a very good day for dad, as mom reported. He and mom had been to his doctor's office for a follow-up visit, and he received a clean bill of health. I actually called the house that afternoon, and did not get an answer, so I immediately thought that he may have had to be admitted once again to the hospital. I called my grandmother for information and clarification. She told me of the doctor's appointment, and said that dad was fine. His doctor had taken him off of some of his medications, and mom reported that he felt good. He and mom had a good dinner and evening together, and things with him were fine. He also had a very memorable visit with his neighbor, Dennis, which brought joy and laughter to his soul.

Mom got up the next day, got dressed, and went into his room to tell him that she was going to the beauty shop. They had been sleeping in separate rooms for a while, since Dad suffered from sleep apnea and used a device to regulate his breathing. As she approached and attempted to awaken him, he lay there still with no movement. There were no breath sounds at all. She said that he was somewhat cold to the touch, and that was when she knew that he was gone. He had slipped away from us in his sleep. The coroner later stated the cause of death to be natural causes which in Dad's case was Cardiac arrest. What a way to leave this earth, peacefully in your sleep. He no longer had to suffer not being able to walk because his feet were so swollen with gout. He no longer had to suffer the tightness in his chest, and wheezing loudly trying to catch a breath. He no longer had to endure long waits at the doctor's office and extended hospital stays. He no longer had to pop pill after pill after pill. His suffering was over and he made it home. God rest his soul.

My sisters, brother and I immediately went to mother's side to assist her with the funeral and burial arrangements. It was very difficult for her; she and dad had been married for 46 years, and had been together for over 50 years. They were high school sweethearts; they were a team and had a long lasting love affair. Mom gained strength from her faith in God. She understood God calling dad home, she was just lonely over the fact that her long time companion was gone. Mom really loved dad and stood by him through sickness and health as well as good times and bad. There union was truly blessed.

Dad's home going service was very nice, and he looked beautiful for he was a handsome and striking man. There were so many people who came out to show their last respects for him. Dad had been retired from Huntsville International Airport for a few years, but he had a shoe shine stand in the lobby of the AmSouth bank building in downtown Huntsville. He loved shining shoes, and did this as a hobby. He needed something to keep him busy and get him out of the house. The bank building housed law firms as well as CPA firms, and dad got to know many of the individuals who were employed by these institutions pretty well. They all spoke of his genuine kindness and goodness, and they held him in high regard. They echoed the point that he had a gigantic heart, and would do anything for anyone. Dad was a Good Samaritan and a real people person.

We were overwhelmed by the pouring out of love and affection that he received, and I am sure that it touched us all in ways that are inconceivable. It made me want to straighten up and to be a better person, a better steward to mankind. It taught me that you do whatever you can for others, because that is God's will. After all, I believe that God put us on this earth to help one another by receiving his blessings. We missed dad immensely since we are such a close family, but we know that his spirit lives on in each and every one of us.

I was still in the middle of my divorce when all of this happened. If I hadn't had such a close relationship with God, I don't know what I would have done. My dad meant the world to me, and every time that I would call he would always greet me as "sweetheart." I just loved it when he called me that, so much that I would wait anxiously to hear him say it each and every time that I phoned home. He was really the only man in my life that I truly believe loved me unconditionally, and now he's gone. I no longer have the love of my dad, and it hurts like hell.

I had to learn to live without dad. I had to learn to call the house, and not ask mother to put him on the phone. I had to go home only to see his empty chair, the chair that he sat in every night to watch the news or some sporting event. I had to go outside to the backyard, and look at all the foliage that he patiently cared for. I had to get up on Sunday morning and walk downstairs to the kitchen, and not read, and discuss news in the Sunday paper with him. I would also miss Dad's request for me to make his favorite appetizer at our family Christmas Eve gatherings.

We all leaned on one another during this time, and found strength and comfort in each other. I went home every other weekend for a couple of months to visit mom. While I was there, I made a point to go sit and visit dad. I found great solace sitting by his grave and pouring out my heart. I felt his presence ever so strongly, and I knew that he was with me in heart, mind and soul. Whenever I have a difficult time, day or circumstance, I call on dad, and there is a warmth or comfort that shrouds me, and I know that I am alright, just as I was as a little girl being held in his arms.

After several months, I sought direction from an attorney and formally filed for divorce. I was profoundly sad; it was difficult saying goodbye to my marriage of over 20 years, as well as the fantasy of living happily ever after. I wondered how I got to this point in my life. I had been married for most of my adult life, and never imagined that I would be a single woman again. What would I do? Where would I live? How would I cope? All of these questions swirled around and around in my mind, and I could deliver no answers. I had committed my life and submitted my-self to a man that I had loved with my whole heart. He was someone whom I had trusted my life with and a man that I would have loved for an eternity.

Things had become very stressful since my husband and I could not agree on a settlement in our divorce. There was also the fact that he remained in the house and refused to move out. The tension and stress was unreal. I was upset all of the time and just wanted all of this to end. I had almost given up on everything and begun to question my faith. I can honestly say that this was the lowest that I had ever felt in my life. I did not want to feel the pain anymore and I had thoughts of things that no one should ever experience. Things such as slitting my wrist; sitting in my car suffocating from carbon monoxide poisoning and a pill overdose. I wanted to stop trying and I wanted to end it all. I needed the pain to go away! I had given up and felt that my life would never be happy again. I would never have the joy or twinkle in my eyes that I once so naturally displayed. I believed that I was on the verge of a nervous breakdown, and it took some serious intervention from God to bring me back.

On my darkest day, I vividly remember dropping to my knees and poring my heart out to God. I cried and asked for direction and substance in my life. I also asked for peace and most of all I begged for his love and mercy. I recall being on my knees for at least 30 minutes or more. Suddenly, calm came from out of nowhere. I felt burden, stress, and anxiety lifted from my soul. God was beside me that day, and everything was good. I felt that I had been touched and all worries were washed away. All of the "stuff" was still there, but somehow it did not really matter anymore. This is the day that I truly began to walk by faith, and to entrust my life, my salvation to God. This was also the day that I honestly forgave my husband. I let it all go, and I forgave him for all of the past hurt and wrong doings. I prayed to God for his soul salvation, and I wished him nothing but peace and happiness.

My brother Joe called me that afternoon, and I discussed my transformation with him. My brother is one year younger than me, and the only boy in the family. He is a handsome young man with the body to match. However, like everyone he has problems and a serious addiction to drugs. His addiction has lasted for well over 20 years. He has also been in and out of rehabilitation centers, and the struggle was ever present in his life. He has been blessed to have had some really good jobs, but they all ended when his drug problem took center stage. Joe was now learning to become a long-haul truck driver. He had always dreamed "big", and wanted those around him to share in his vision. My family and I were happy that he would no longer dwell in one place for too long; maybe this would deter his problem.

Joe and I spoke often and he knew fully what was going on in my life. He was a good listener, and really cared for my well being. Since he has struggled with addiction for all of his adult life, he was self-removed from many family gatherings and therefore not as close to our family as he would have liked. None the less, he had become a kind and gentle man. He cares for my girls and me, and since the passing of our dad, he has stepped up to the plate, so to speak. He is now the head of the family, and wants to prove to us that we can count on him.

14

God's Divine Mercy

My dear, sweet mother has been cancer free for eight years now. She had suffered from breast cancer, and had undergone a mastectomy to remove her left breast. It was May and time for the American Cancer Society's "Relay for Life" walk. It was the very first year that I had been able to participate. Mom was the captain of her church sponsored team, so it meant a lot to me that I "show up" and walk on her behalf.

Earlier in the week after wearing a new pair of shoes, I had turned and slightly twisted my ankle. I'd had similar injuries before while on my high school and college dance teams, so I knew the symptoms well. The pain from the sprain was moderate, so I thought that I could walk a few laps and call it a night. I got out there on that track, and the adrenalin began to flow. I also felt a great sense of pride knowing that I was part of something so special. So I kept on walking and walking and walking. The next thing I knew, it was 6 o'clock in the morning, and I had made 60 trips around the track which equates to 15 miles, the most on our team.

The ankle felt fine, as long as I was moving, but as soon as I stopped it really hurt badly. The next few days brought about so much pain. I could barely walk the day after the event, and simply hobbled along my way. That next week I noticed that my ankle was blue and black with significant swelling. I began to ice my ankle, and keep it elevated as much as possible, but the pain never went away. Instead, it began to travel up my leg. At first it was in my lower leg, then my calf, and up my inner thigh and eventually to my groin area. My leg was red, swollen, and hot to the touch. It was then that I knew that something was wrong; I had that gut feeling once again.

One afternoon, I was lying on the floor doing my sit ups after working out to a Billy Blanks Tae Bo tape. I changed the television channel to watch the remaining half hour of the Oprah Winfrey show. As I continued with my sit ups a story came on about a man who had problems with his foot. He, like me, did not think anything about it at first; he simply thought it was a slight injury. Well, the story ended in the man finally going to the doctor, and having his foot amputated. This gentleman had a rare disease, or cancer that was in its advanced stages. I sat up, and thought to myself, "Oh my God, are you trying to tell me something?" I felt like God had intended me to see this story since it came on right after I took out the exercise tape. I immediately sprang to my feet, grabbed my day timer, and called my doctor to make an appointment.

When I saw the doctor a couple of days later, I explained to him what had happened to me. He examined my leg, and noticed that my ankle was blue and black. He asked me how long it had been since I had sustained the injury and I told him approximately three weeks. He looked at me, and asked, "Why did you wait so long before coming to see me?" My initial reply was that I did not think that it was serious, and after looking up my symptoms on the internet I had self diagnosed my injury as being a torn ligament. I continued by telling him that it wasn't until the pain began to travel up my leg that I became alarmed. He told me that he was going to send me to have an ultrasound of my leg, as well as an x-ray of my ankle. I left his office, and immediately went to have these tests performed.

I made it to the imaging center that same afternoon, and as the technician was performing the ultrasound she kept focusing on my groin area as well as the area behind my knee. She would not tell me what she was looking for, or had found, but after about 30 minutes the tests were complete. She asked me to wait, and later informed me that I needed to take the film of the ultrasound back to my doctor's office that day. I thought that it was a strange request, and knew that the technician had identified something on the ultrasound. I was very nervous, and could not begin to imagine what it possibly could be. With film in hand, I returned to my doctor's office.

Again, I sat in the same examination room from earlier that day waiting to get the news. Mareva was with me, and she was anxious to find out as well. My doctor appeared, and he came right to the point telling me that I had two blood clots in my leg. One was in my groin area, and the other behind the knee of my left leg. He called it a Deep Venous Thrombosis or "DVT" which meant that it was in the deep or interior vein of my body. I had heard of a DVT before, so I knew that it was serious. My doctor pointed out that people sometimes die from this particular type of blood clot. He also went on to tell me that the NBC reporter, David Bloom, who was covering the war in Iraq died from a DVT. It is possible that the clots could travel to your heart and/or lungs, and cause sudden death.

I was horrified upon hearing this news. I could not believe that I had "two" of these potentially life threatening clots in my body. How could such a small injury escalate into a major health crisis? My doctor exited the room to contact a vascular surgeon, whom he would refer me to for further treatment. The surgeon was not available, so I was told to go home and wait for further instruction. Before leaving, I asked my doctor about the course of treatment, and his reply was that I would be put on a blood thinner immediately, and that it may be necessary to spend a night or two in the hospital. He concluded by saying that the vascular surgeon would speak to me in depth to answer all of my questions and address my concerns.

I left his office feeling scared to death; I did not want to move. I could not wrap my brain around the fact that I had been doing everything (exercising, carrying Lauren up and down the stairs, washing the van, and cleaning the house, etc …) while these ticking time bombs lay in wait in my blood stream. I also recall thanking God, because he was the only reason I was still alive. He has kept me from all hurt, harm, and danger for the second time. First it was my heart scare, and now two blood clots. As I drove home all I could do was say, "Thank You, Lord" over and over again. That night as I prayed, I had a long conversation with God. I told him that he has my full attention, and that I am listening and waiting to do whatever it is that he wants me to do. The power of God is truly awesome.

I was summoned to the hospital the next day. The vascular surgeon's office was my first stop. A nurse explained to me that I was going to be admitted for a 24 hour period, primarily to be monitored as a blood thinning medication was introduced into my blood stream. The nurse continued by telling me that I would take Coumadin (a blood thinning medication) for approximately 4–6 months and that I would need to take it easy and stay off of my feet for the next 3–4 days. When the vascular surgeon appeared, he just sat and looked at me in silence. He uttered these words, "You are a very lucky woman," over and over again. He said that my clots were in the deep venous region of my leg, and that they could have easily traveled to my heart or lungs. My reply to him was, "I am blessed, not lucky, but truly blessed."

I was admitted to the hospital, and treatment began immediately. First, I had to have blood drawn. A nurse entered my room, and drew over a dozen vials of blood for testing. I was then asked to watch a video on how to administer self injections. I was to inject a drug by the name of Lovenox into my abdomen twice a day for an indefinite period of time. I was released the following day with a prescription for the Lovenox, as well as one for Coumadin. The drugs work hand in hand to prevent blood clots. I was told to stay away from certain types of food since they counteract the effectiveness of the drugs. Secondly, I was also told to be very careful, any serious accident to any limb of my body could cause me to bleed to death. Both drugs work to thin the blood, and my body may not be able to clot and stop the bleeding. Furthermore, I would have to get my blood checked once a week to make sure that I had an adequate amount of the drugs in my system. I could tell that it was going to be a long six months!

Just as I was getting accustomed to giving my self shots and popping pills, I had to direct my attention to Lauren. Once again she needed hip surgery. This time it was her right hip that was partially dislocated. She also needed to have pins and plates from her surgery five years ago removed. All of this would mean six weeks in a full body cast in the height of the summer heat.

Now, I really felt like God was testing me, and putting my feet to the fire. I didn't know how much more that I could stand. It seemed that a problem, circumstance or situation followed me wherever I went. I felt like I was going to break. I listed them one by one. First it was the death of my father, the long process of divorce, two blood clots, and now Lauren's hip surgery. Truly, if it weren't for my faith, where would I be and where would I be going? I told myself that had I not known sorrow, despair, desperation, angst, suffering, and strife that I would not recognize the good, wonderful and awesome life that was waiting for me. I would look for, and one day find my peace, and joy in the morning.

Lauren's surgery went well. She experienced a few post surgical complications, but after five days in the hospital she and I were sent home. The time seemed to fly, except for the days that she was downright miserable because of the summer heat. Her cast was removed just before the beginning of the new school year. She was really stiff and sore, therefore her doctor prescribed physical therapy immediately to assist in her post operative care. As the weeks went by she loosened up slowly, but she was still having problems sleeping. It was common practice to get up with her during the course of the night and re-position her body, but now she was waking up five to six times a night because she just could not get comfortable. She and I were both miserable!

Something that really kept me going during this time was my brother Joe sending me inspirational greeting cards. They seemed to come on a day when my faith was being tested. He would also enclose what he called a "love offering", of various amounts of money. I never asked him for money, but he knew that my salary was very meek and therefore did it out of the goodness of his heart. He told me that he found these cards out on the road driving from state to state. They were very special, and I have kept each and everyone of them in a scrap book to remind me of the times.

My divorce mediation hearing was the first week in October, 2006, and we finally reached a settlement. We will need to sign final papers, and appear before a judge, but I am in prayer that this will happen within the next 60 days. We both remain in the house until it is put on the market and sold; hopefully it will be sooner than later. I think that God was trying to teach me a lesson about patience. I always knew that I possessed such an attribute, but this would be my real test.

I also received some other good news. My blood clots are beginning to age which meant that they are adhering to the walls of the veins and thus less likely to break off and travel. I was also told to discontinue taking my daily dosage of Coumadin and my weekly visits to the lab for the collection, and testing of my blood could cease. This news was a wonderful and bountiful blessing.

15

The Consumption of Grief

I had been given the news that my mother was having surgery in a few days. She had a nodule on her lung in an area that cannot be reached for a biopsy, so her physician had opted to remove it instead. After it was removed, the nodule would be tested for malignancy, and she would find out if further treatment would be required. She had been a smoker for most of her life so the news was not surprising, but still very alarming.

The surgery went well except for the fact that Mom developed a blood clot as well as a touch of pneumonia. The good news was that the nodule was small, and non-cancerous. What a relief! Her stay in the hospital was prolonged due to the complications, thus making for a longer recovery period. Upon her release she was in good spirits, and looking forward to getting back on her feet. All I could say was, "To God be the glory!"

Thanksgiving was near, and the girls and I planned a trip to Huntsville to visit the family. It would be nice to see everyone, especially Mom, since I had not been able to visit her since the surgery.

Beverly along with my grandmother prepared our Thanksgiving feast. It was customary for everyone to pitch in to prepare the meal, but Mom was just not feeling well enough to assist. The menu was established and the food prepared. We were truly blessed to partake of such a wonderful feast.

Being home was therapeutic, and it gave me the opportunity to reconnect with family and friends, which was the perfect antidote to my marital woes. It was difficult in the sense that I love cooking, and preparing my dining room table for such holidays as Thanksgiving and Christmas. I hated the fact that I could not sit down with my husband and children, at our home to give thanks for all that had been given to us. Holidays are always sentimental, and a special time to share with family and friends.

This Thanksgiving was strange in the fact that dad was not with us this year. If he were still alive he would have most certainly prepared the best fried turkey in town. Dad liked to barbecue and use his deep fryer. I loved to watch him prepare the seasonings for the meats. He would be ever so careful in marinating the chicken, ribs, turkey or whatever he was cooking. There was a certain amount of time that it took to make the meat flavorful, and perfect for consumption. Also, no one else could do this but him. Mom would offer her assistance, but he ultimately would tell her to stand aside, that this was his undertaking. Not only was his cooking missed but, of course, his overall presence. Mom had a terrible time dealing with his absence. All she did was sit in his chair day and night, day after day. She looked so sad and pitiful. I had never seen my mother in such a state. This woman, who was full of vim and vigor, was wasting away before my very eyes. At first glance one would think that she had lost her zest for life, and that she wanted to join the love of her life.

It is not uncommon for one spouse to grieve so much that they die of a broken heart. Friends have described the sad tale of one parent dying, only to have the other parent follow suit months later. Would this happen in my family? Would this be the destiny of my parents? I understood that mom was not feeling well as she was recuperating from surgery; but she was in a bona fide state of depression. How long would this last, and what would it take to get her out of this state?

I gave the situation a lot of thought. Should I confront her with my fears, just leave her alone to work it out by herself, or should I call a sibling meeting for immediate intervention? I chose the latter and we subtly asked her about her mood and state of mind. Her reply was sharp and swift. She expressed an indescribable feeling of loneliness, and further went on to say that she would deal with it in her time frame and not ours. She concluded the conversation by stating her desire not to talk about this anymore. So, we left her alone, and prayed that God would continue to be with her and keep her.

The Christmas season rolled around, and there was mom once again sitting just as she had done one month prior. It was a family tradition to get together and open gifts on Christmas Eve. Although everyone was feeling quite somber over dad's absence, we managed little by little to celebrate the birth of our Lord and Savior, Jesus Christ.

It had been exactly one month since I had last laid eyes on mom, and she did not appear to show any improvement at all. She had lost a lot of weight and had become a hermit. I was really concerned at this point, and did not waste time with a "town meeting." I cut to the chase with her, and disclosed all of my deepest fears.

I told her that I needed her, and hated to see her in this awful state. She had been my rock while I was going through the divorce, and she had always been the one to take care of the girls when I was sick or hospitalized. I also told her to fight and to keep going for her grandchildren, that they need her. I concluded my tirade by saying that dad would not want her to give up on living, that he would want her to carry on his legacy and memory. We both shed tears, and she assured me that she wanted to live. She stated that she was having a difficult time because the holidays were always a big deal to dad. How he had loved for the family to assemble at their home!

We all put on brave faces, and continued with the festivities, just as we had in the past. The girls enjoyed opening gifts as we celebrated the birth of Jesus. We visited extended family members, got together to tell of stories, enjoyed a cup of egg nog here and there, and prayed to see yet another holiday season.

I felt dad's presence, and knew that he was in heaven looking down on his family with a smile upon his face. I knew that he was happy that we did not let his home going cast a shadow over the celebration of the season. He would want us to continue all of our family holiday traditions.

Upon my departure that Christmas of 2006, I felt saddened by the fact that mom was having such a difficult time. Would she ever be able to deal with dad's passing? Would she learn to live as a single woman? Would she be accustomed to doing things and going places alone? How would she fill the void in the house, as well as in her heart? I truly believe the adage that time heals wounds, but only God knows how much time she will need. I continue to pray for my mother.

16

Rebirth: The Road to a new Beginning

The drive home from Huntsville was routine with little fanfare, as the weather was ideal for the three hour trip and the traffic flow was light. Upon getting out of the car after arriving home I felt a throbbing sensation in my right foot. It was very painful to stand and walk but I had to get Lauren and our belongings out of the car. As I unpacked that evening I noticed that my foot was slightly swollen. I surmised that I had been on my feet too long, and this was the price I had to pay.

Occasionally, during summer, winter and spring break I worked for my Allstate agent, Larry. Since it was winter break and we were out of school, Larry had asked me to work a few days after the Christmas holiday. The work was not hard as I primarily accepted and applied payments. I also answered the telephone, and performed light-duty filing.

The following day, as I got out of bed to prepare for work I stood up, and immediately fell to the floor. What was happening to me? I pulled myself up on the bed, but I could not bear any weight on my right foot. I sat there on the edge of the bed examining my foot, and it was enormous in size. How in the world could it have swollen so much overnight? I pushed on it, and my entire foot and ankle were as puffy as a cushion. I kept trying to walk, but I was in excruciating pain. I fought back the tears, and cleared my mind, trying to figure out what I should do next.

I hobbled into Mareva's room and grabbed the heating pad. I applied the heat for about ten minutes and once again attempted to stand. At this point I could bear some weight, but it was still very painful. I considered calling "911", but then I thought it would be silly to do so since this was probably nothing serious. Maybe I'd had too much exercise and activity over the last couple of weeks. I managed to shower, get dressed, and go to work. I took a couple of Advil tablets for the pain, and went about my day. I was limping and it still hurt to bear weight, but I kept on going.

Later that evening and the days following, the pain and swelling worsened. I knew that I needed to have this checked out so I finally called my doctor to make an appointment. Since it was the holiday season my doctor had taken some time off, therefore I was seen by the nurse practitioner.

She asked me a series of questions, ranging from if I had sustained an injury, was I bitten by an insect, etc … My answer was an emphatic "no" to all of her questions. She then sat down; looked at me and said, "I think you may have another blood clot." I was speechless. I never imagined that I would hear those words again. How could this even be possible since my first clot was in my left leg and now the right leg was hurting? Can blood clots travel in this manner?

Of course, the nurse practitioner could not answer my questions as this was merely a suspicion on her part. She knew that I was alarmed, and wanted answers so she instructed me to go back to the vascular surgeon who had treated my clots last spring.

As I drove to my next appointment with the vascular surgeon I could not help thinking, "How could this be? What are the chances of this happening yet again?" I had been given a clean bill of health a few months prior, so why did it feel like I was trapped in a time warp?

So many thoughts ran through my mind as I tried so valiantly not to succumb to the fear that I felt. I was scared to death of what the doctor would discover. What else could it be other than the reoccurrence of a blood clot? I called home to notify Mareva of the events of the day. I also explained to her that I had other tests to be performed. She told me not to worry and to pray. I am so blessed to have such a caring child; she has grown up so much, and was blossoming into a wonderful human being.

I arrived at the vascular surgeon's office, and it was all too familiar. An ultrasound was performed on my right leg and there it was, another DVT. I could not believe it, and asked the technician to please double check her findings. I explained to her that I was here just months prior with this same diagnosis in the other leg and she was bewildered. She, as well as I, could not believe that I could be in this situation once more. Again, I did not have any of the normal symptoms of someone who was prone to clotting. I was not an elderly person; I was not overweight, a smoker or a diabetic. These are the normal factors which one associates with blood clots.

A nurse escorted me to the hospital admittance desk, which was just over the cat walk from my doctor's office. I remember sitting in that hospital bed crying uncontrollably. How did I get here and how long would all of this last? As usual I was alone; no one to hold my hand to reassure me that everything would be okay. My blood pressure was elevated, and my heart was pounding out of control.

Eventually, I managed to calm down and assess what was going on. I made phone calls to Mareva, my sisters and Francina. Both Beverly and Cathy wanted to come and be by my side, but I told them that it was not necessary. Francina came to the hospital with her bible, CD player, and CD's in hand. She knew from our phone conversation that I was somewhat panicked, so she brought the word in whatever medium that was at her disposal to my bedside for my comfort.

My doctor finally came to my room and explained what my stay would encompass. He told me that I would need to stay for a couple of days to be monitored in order to insure that my blood was being thinned. I began the regimen of Coumadin as well as injections of Lovenox on a daily basis. He also told me that I was going to be referred to a Hematologist/Oncologist for further treatment, since he did not know why the blood clots kept occurring. A Hematologist, of course, studies blood disorders. Did I have some type of blood abnormality or condition?

A nurse told me that I would need to have my blood tested for abnormalities and/or disorders, so she sat down over a dozen glass vials on my bed to be filled, and sent out to the lab. I felt as if I were at the Red Cross donating blood since so much was being taken out of my arm. I would have to wait on the results of these tests and put it in the hands of the Lord.

After Francina left I began to listen to the CD's, and read the word from her frayed and tattered bible. I knew that her bible had brought her through many fearful and fretful nights. I prayed to God for forgiveness, since I had not once stopped to thank him for sparing my life yet again. Here I am walking around with this potentially deadly blood clot in my leg, and all I could think about was "poor me" and have pity on myself. God keeps giving me these chances at life, so I need to grab, embrace and hold on to all that I am taking away from these experiences. I must understand it for myself in hopes that I can help others, I need to know that I can make a difference to someone else and be a blessing in their life.

I need to speak to the parents who are holding vigil over their premature infants at the local hospital. I need to reach out to the woman who has discovered and unveiled her husband's indiscretions. I need to reach out to the care giver who devotes his or her life to their loved one who cannot care for themselves. I need to seek out anyone who is trying to understand, and cope with the sudden loss of a parent, a mentor and a friend. I need to pray for the person who receives a frightening diagnosis and prognosis from their physician.

I had much work to do. I didn't have time to lie around and wallow in misery. I was so exhausted, and in many ways thought that God knew that I needed a break. I brought in the New Year lying there in that hospital bed alone with no one to cheer in the coming of 2007. At that moment, the strike of midnight, I realized that it did not matter that I had no one by my side. I was alright with being alone. I ushered in 2007 talking to God, praying and asking for guidance, he has always been by my side and that was fine with me. I felt such calm and peace at that moment in time, and I knew that the Holy Spirit was present in that space.

It is worth mentioning that there was a stained glass window in my room, and it lit up like a light fixture by the flick of a switch. It was something to behold, stunning, and beautiful. During my stay I inquired about the light as no other room contained such an exquisite object. A nurse informed me that my room was part of the old hospital chapel that had recently been relocated within the hospital.

This explained why I felt such peace and solitude being hospitalized this time around. There was much tranquility in the confines of those walls, and what a wonderful blessing to have received. As I walked out of that room upon my release, I looked back at that window, and uttered the words, "Thank you."

I finally received lab results from the hematologist and the diagnosis of a blood abnormality or deficiency was stated. I was told that this was nothing to worry about if closely monitored and managed. He also mentioned that this was not uncommon and that many people live with blood clots. I would now have to remain on Coumadin indefinitely and have my blood checked regularly. Again, I was just happy to be alive.

As in past years, I had scheduled doctor's appointments for annual checkups at the beginning of the year. My physical with my general practitioner was uneventful, except for the fact that I received considerable scolding for not seeking treatment for my leg upon the onset of pain. My doctor sternly made it known to me that I could not afford to sit around with a "wait and see" attitude. In the future I am to go to the hospital emergency room immediately, as it may be a matter of life or death.

My gynecological visit was alarming in that I was suspected of having uterine fibroids. My doctor suggested that I undergo an ultra sound for a concrete diagnosis. I felt as if my body was falling apart, but why? I work out regularly, I eat properly and I try very hard to take care of myself. What else would I have to deal with, what was next?

I felt like finding a hole to crawl into so that I could cry myself into oblivion. Where is all of this stuff coming from and when would I find any resemblance of normalcy in my life? Am I not truly walking by faith?

The results of the ultra sound came back and sure enough it showed that I had a very large fibroid. A uterine fibroid is a non-cancerous tumor of the uterus. Upon hearing this news I sat down with my doctor to discuss options in dealing with the fibroid. We both felt that due to the fact that I am in my early forties and not wanting to have any more children, that I should have a partial hysterectomy. He would perform the procedure laprascopically, and only remove my uterus. My ovaries and cervix would be left in tact, thus no need for hormone therapy.

I left my doctor's office armed with all of the information necessary to make such an important decision in my life. I would no longer be able to bear fruit, would it make me feel less of a woman? I had been blessed with two beautiful girls so I have no regrets, no complaints, and there was no looking back. After all, I am soon to be a single woman anyway. I am not in a relationship, and very seriously doubt that I would be in one any time soon. The decision was a relatively easy one to make as I decided to go ahead with the surgery.

Wow, I would be turning "44" soon and, as usual, my sister Beverly and her husband Burl hosted a birthday party in my honor. It was just the pick-me-up that I needed. I was beginning to get depressed again, since the divorce was dragging out. It was almost a year and a half ago that I began sleeping in the guest room. When would I begin to live my life again? I am in a holding pattern indefinitely.

The party was awesome in that many of my family members attended, as well as friends. I had a handful of childhood friends, and sorority sisters (AKA's) in attendance. They all mean so much to me, and seeing each of them made my evening so very special. Forty-Four felt good, and I eagerly await the celebration of many years to come. I thanked God for all of these blessings.

Surgery day approached, and surprisingly I was not scared at all. I just knew that everything would be alright. I had prayed, and felt in my heart that God had already answered my prayers. Mom came to accompany me to the hospital and to stay for a few days. My doctor had pointed out that the total recovery period for such a procedure is five to six weeks. Therefore, Beverly and Cathy had committed themselves, to doing whatever was needed of them during this time. My main concern was who would take care of Lauren? She is so dependant on others for her daily care.

My family and church members assured me that she would be alright, and that they would take excellent care of her. With all of that said I set that concern aside and focused on the issue at hand.

On March 6, 2007, I had my uterus removed via laparoscopy. I woke up and asked the nurse what happened? His reply was simply "Your surgery went well." I tried to touch and feel my abdomen, but I was still very heavily sedated from the anesthetic. I was relieved to know that I didn't have yet another cut on my body. There are two small incisions to the right and left of my navel, and a tiny incision in my navel itself. All of these marks, cuts and scars on my body are badges of honor, and I learned to wear them well. I was proud of each and every one of them, for they each had a profound story to tell.

I was released and able to go home the following day. My doctor informed me that the fibroid was twice the size of my uterus, and that it had calcified. He explained that it was so hard, that it took two blades to chop it up before it could be removed. I knew that on occasion, I could feel it protruding from my lower abdomen, and it was pressing on my bladder. He continued to say that he was pleased that I decided to have the surgery now instead of waiting. If he was pleased, then you know that I was elated to get that enormous mass out of my body!

The next few weeks brought about rest and recuperation from the surgery. I was so very thankful that it went well. By the second week I felt really good, but knew that I had to continue to take it easy, and let my body heal. So many of my family members and friends brought over food, called, and sent flowers and cards. I felt blessed to have so many people care for me, and offer to be there for me and to lend a helping hand.

During this time we finally put our home on the market to sell. I also signed final divorce papers, and had my day in court. After twenty-one years of marriage I am now a single woman. It appears that issues are culminating. My girls are well and thriving, which makes my world alright. It has been approximately one and a half years since my husband and I separated. What has been so very difficult is the fact that we have continued to dwell in the same house; he still insists on staying until it sells. The tension is unthinkable, and I would not wish it on anyone. I am relieved, as burdens are slowly being lifted. I can see a flicker of light at the end of the tunnel. I can see a piece of gold at the end of the rainbow and I can see two set of footprints in the sand as God is not carrying me anymore but allowing me to stand and walk on my own. Now I know what my church member meant when she said that God favors me. There is safety in his care, and he is my covering. He has been taking care of me all of this time, and what an awesome gift to behold.

Have I finally arrived? Has my faith become my barometer? My pastor Rev. Amos Williams, Jr. always preaches to his congregation about walking like God, and living a spiritual life, about doing the right thing, and caring for others. He speaks of sowing good seeds and waiting for a magnificent harvest.

Pastor Williams posed these questions to his congregation, "What do you do, and where do you go when you are discouraged?" Where does one find encouragement?

In bad times do you let your flesh be your guide? Do you dwell in wrong doing until it gets the best of you? Or do you make the decision to turn to God for help?

God uses us to help others through our testimony of faith and healing. We should not be so consumed with our lives and things of this world that we cannot take the time to reach out and help another. It is my sincere prayer that the words on these pages touch the heart and souls of many; to know that with God all things are possible. Reach out for him, trust in him, and let him guide you into eternity.

I now know that my calling in life is to work with children, especially those who need a little extra care. I want to be the hands, the eyes, the legs, and the mouth for those without the ability to use their own. God has granted me patience to love, care, and nurture these beings that he so lovingly created.

Throughout the past few years, I have been on a journey. When I have been faced with a crisis I have prayed about it, and let God lead me to my decisions. I know that he has been preparing me to step into my future, and to walk into my inheritance. I now stand here strong, with my arms stretched out wide, ministering and testifying about his love and what he has done for me. The struggle is difficult but when prayers go up, blessings come down.

The End!

978-0-595-47186-7
0-595-47186-2